Reference Services
for the Unserved

Forthcoming topics in *The Reference Librarian* series:

• The Roles of Reference Librarians: Today and Tomorrow, Number 54

Published:

Reference Services for the Unserved has also been published as *The Reference Librarian*, Number 53 1996.

The development, preparation, and publication of this work has been undertaken with great care. However, the publisher, employees, editors, and agents of The Haworth Press and all imprints of The Haworth Press, Inc., including the Haworth Medical Press and Pharmaceutical Products Press, are not responsible for any errors contained herein or for consequences that may ensue from use of materials or information contained in this work. Opinions expressed by the author(s) are not necessarily those of The Haworth Press, Inc.

The Haworth Press, Inc., 10 Alice Street, Binghamton, NY 13904-1580 USA

Library of Congress Cataloging-in-Publication Data

Reference services for the unserved / Fay Zipkowitz, editor.
     p. cm.
Includes bibliographical references (p.) and index.
ISBN 1-56024-797-5 (alk. paper)
    1. Libraries and the mentally ill–United States. 2. Libraries and abused women–United States. 3. Libraries and readers–United States–Bibliography. I. Zipkowitz, Fay.
Z711.92.M42R44 1996   95-46713
027.6--dc20   CIP

Reference Services for the Unserved

Fay Zipkowitz
Editor

The Haworth Press, Inc.
New York · London

INDEXING & ABSTRACTING

Contributions to this publication are selectively indexed or abstracted in print, electronic, online, or CD-ROM version(s) of the reference tools and information services listed below. This list is current as of the copyright date of this publication. See the end of this section for additional notes.

- *Academic Abstracts/CD-ROM,* EBSCO Publishing, P.O. Box 2250, Peabody, MA 01960-7250

- *Academic Search: data base of 2,000 selected academic serials. updated monthly: EBSCO Publishing, 83 Pine Street, Peabody, Ma 01960,* EBSCO Publishing, 83 Pine Street, Peabody, MA 10960

- *Current Awareness Bulletin,* Association for Information Management, Information House, 20-24 Old Street, London EC1V 9AP, England

- *Current Index to Journals in Education,* Syracuse University, 4-194 Center for Science and Technology, Syracuse, NY 13244-4100

- *Educational Administration Abstracts (EAA),* Sage Publications, Inc., 2455 Teller Road, Newbury Park, CA 91320

- *IBZ International Bibliography of Periodical Literature,* Zeller Verlag GmbH & Co., P.O.B. 1949, d-49009 Osnabruck, Germany

- *Index to Periodical Articles Related to Law,* University of Texas, 727 East 26th Street, Austin, TX 78705

- *Information Science Abstracts,* Plenum Publishing Company, 233 Spring Street, New York, NY 10013-1578

- *Informed Librarian, The,* Infosources Publishing, 140 Norma Road, Teaneck, NJ 07666

- *INSPEC Information Services,* Institution of Electrical Engineers, Michael Faraday House, Six Hills Way, Stevenage, Herts SG1 2AY, England

(continued)

- *INTERNET ACCESS (& additional networks) Bulletin Board for Libraries ("BUBL"), coverage of information resources on INTERNET, JANET, and other networks.*
  - JANET X.29: UK.AC.BATH.BUBL or 00006012101300
  - TELNET: BUBL.BATH.AC.UK or 138.38.32.45 login 'bubl'
  - Gopher: BUBL.BATH.AC.UK (138.32.32.45). Port 7070
  - World Wide Web: http: / / www.bubl.bath.ac.uk./BUBL/ home.html
  - NISSWAIS: telnetniss.ac.uk (for the NISS gateway)
  The Andersonian Library, Curran Building, 101 St. James Road, Glasgow G4 ONS, Scotland

- *Library & Information Science Abstracts (LISA),* Bowker-Saur Limited, Maypole House, Maypole Road, East Grinstead, West Sussex, RH19 1HH England

- *Library Literature,* The H.W. Wilson Company, 950 University Avenue, Bronx, NY 10452

- *MasterFILE: updated database from EBSCO Publishing, 83 Pine Street, Peabody, Ma 01960,* EBSCO Publishing, 83 Pine Street, Peabody, Ma 01960

- *Newsletter of Library and Information Services,* China Sci-Tech Book Review, Library of Academia Sinica, 8 Kexueyuan Nanlu, Zhongguancun, Beijing 100080, People's Republic of China

- *OT BibSys,* American Occupational Therapy Foundation, P.O. Box 31220, Bethesda, MD 20824-1220

- *Referativnyi Zhurnal (Abstracts Journal of the Institute of Scientific Information of the Republic of Russia),* The Institute of Scientific Information, Baltijskaja ul., 14, Moscow A-219, Republic of Russia

- *Sage Public Administration Abstracts (SPAA),* Sage Publications, Inc., 2455 Teller Road, Newbury Park, CA 91320

(continued)

SPECIAL BIBLIOGRAPHIC NOTES

related to special journal issues (separates)
and indexing/abstracting

- ☐ indexing/abstracting services in this list will also cover material in any "separate" that is co-published simultaneously with Haworth's special thematic journal issue or DocuSerial. Indexing/abstracting usually covers material at the article/chapter level.

- ☐ monographic co-editions are intended for either non-subscribers or libraries which intend to purchase a second copy for their circulating collections.

- ☐ monographic co-editions are reported to all jobbers/wholesalers/approval plans. The source journal is listed as the "series" to assist the prevention of duplicate purchasing in the same manner utilized for books-in-series.

- ☐ to facilitate user/access services all indexing/abstracting services are encouraged to utilize the co-indexing entry note indicated at the bottom of the first page of each article/chapter/contribution.

- ☐ this is intended to assist a library user of any reference tool (whether print, electronic, online, or CD-ROM) to locate the monographic version if the library has purchased this version but not a subscription to the source journal.

- ☐ individual articles/chapters in any Haworth publication are also available through the Haworth Document Delivery Services (HDDS).

Reference Services for the Unserved

CONTENTS

ABOUT THE EDITOR

Fay Zipkowitz, MSLS, DA, is Professor in the Graduate School of Library and Information Studies at the University of Rhode Island in Kingston. She is a leading authority on the subject of meeting the reference needs of underserved populations.

Introduction:
Library Services to Unserved Populations

Fay Zipkowitz

The last decade has seen unprecedented change in the demand for services to a variety of populations not visible in our libraries before. Their visibility is due in large measure to recognition of their existence at all, and legislation to promote education programs to mainstream disabled children in public schools, deinstitutional-ization of mentally and developmentally disabled people, commu-nity based residents and workshops, service to disabled college students, workplace accommodation, are just a few of the actions which have begun to transform the lives of disabled and challenged people, and to create new challenges for the library community.

Traditionally, libraries are relatively passive places in terms of providing services, not for a lack of will but usually for a lack of funds. Developing outreach services is an expensive process; dem-onstration grant funding is scarce or nonexistent; documenting need is time-consuming and takes time away from other equally impor-tant services. And at the same time, librarians are uneasy when they recognize that there are new constituents in the community or in their user population whose needs they are not adequately meeting,

Fay Zipkowitz is Professor and Interim Director, Graduate School of Library and Information Studies, University of Rhode Island, Kingston, RI 02881-0815. Email: FAYZEE@Uriacc.URI.Edu. Dr. Zipkowitz teaches and researches in library services to special populations, public library services, library administra-tion and professional ethics.

[Haworth co-indexing entry note]: "Introduction: Library Services to Unserved Populations." Zip-kowitz, Fay. Co-published simultaneously in *The Reference Librarian* (The Haworth Press, Inc.) No. 53, 1996, pp. 1-4; and: *Reference Services for the Unserved* (ed: Fay Zipkowitz) The Haworth Press, Inc., 1996, pp. 1-4. Single or multiple copies of this article are available from The Haworth Document Delivery Service: [1-800-342-9678, 9:00 a.m. - 5:00 p.m. (EST)].

and about whom they may not know very much. At a time of shrinking budgets, they are being asked to, and want to, do more.

Many people in these hitherto unserved populations have very specific needs and bring with them some specific limitations in their ability to take advantage of existing library services.

- They may be physically unable to utilize traditional information services.
- They may be educationally unprepared to make use of information resources and services.
- They may be unsocialized or unaccustomed to the settings, expectations and situations we have grown up with and take for granted.
- They may not have the context in which to frame their information requests. They may not know what they need to know.
- They may have a history of frustrating experiences which presents a barrier to dialogue with structured organizations like libraries.

This list could go on, but two points must be emphasized: (1) They are individuals with individual as well as collective needs, and (2) Our commitment to equitable library service to all of our constituent user groups requires that we find ways to meet these needs.

Pressures for services to unserved populations are also coming from parent organizations (academic, school systems, municipal, state, etc.) without, of course, concomitant funding to provide for the planning and implementation of new programs.

This volume brings together research and descriptions of several attempts to meet the information needs of hitherto unserved populations.

Thomas E. Hecker, coordinator of Disabilities Services for the University of Kentucky Libraries, explores approaches to services for patrons with mental illness from two models–patrons with disabilities (whom we may not have encountered before) or problem patrons (with whom we have a long history). He examines the issues of behavior "inappropriate in the situation" and ways of coming to terms with this behavior in order to carry out our professional objectives–providing access to information, improving quality life and meeting the legal mandates of ADA.

Katy Lenn of the University of Oregon Libraries discusses ways of addressing the needs of disabled students in the academic library. She emphasizes that the information needs of disabled students are not different from those of traditional students; the differences are means of access, overcoming barriers to access, and the need for adaptive technologies and techniques.

In undertaking their research on the information needs of battered women, Patricia Dewdney, Roma M. Harris and Christina Lockerby have focused on a population only recently recognized in society, and suggest ways the library professionals can serve them and their support systems. These latter are community based, rather than institution based–social service providers and public policy or decision makers. Dewdney, Harris and Lockerby make specific suggestions, based on the results of their studies, on how public libraries can more effectively respond to battered women; some of these suggestions may also be useful for public libraries planning outreach or response to other unserved population groups.

Integrating technology into a library setting forms the basis for the report by Adele L. Barsh and Meliza Jackson. Their work in the patients' library at the Western Psychiatric Institute and Clinic involved the improvement of access to information sources on behalf of people with cognitive disorders whose ability to process text-based information is impaired. Again, this project and its results may provide some guidance to the use of computer assistance in other settings with other special needs patrons.

Rashelle S. Karp and Patricia L. Horne have surveyed a wide range of unserved population needs, research and application models, identification of successful solutions, and have provided an annotated bibliography of particularly useful material from a variety of sources.

There are many unsung heroes among libraries and librarians who are steadily finding ways to respond to individuals who comprise unserved populations in libraries. Many libraries have made special efforts within their settings to work with other community or campus agencies to solve common problems. The capacity of computers to augment traditional approaches to information access is enabling librarians and teachers to create innovative techniques for disabled patrons. As the technologies become more refined and affordable, more libraries will be able to utilize and customize them to create new access paths for their patrons. This is an exciting prospect, and one of the areas in which librarians may feel more needed rather than threatened.

All of the articles in this volume, and all of the successful approaches to serving unserved populations, rely on strong administrative support. Without wholesale endorsement, planning and recognition by Administrators and funding agencies, librarians will be strictly hampered in their efforts, and easily discouraged. The support must come as strongly and as universally as it did for beginning library services in the first place, for we are creating new services and new access modes for people, just as library pioneers did. And the challenge will not be met by success with one or two groups of newly served patrons–more will be at our doors soon after.

The authors and editor of this volume hope we have provided information, guidance and inspiration to our readers and colleagues in their work with their users, and that unserved populations may be absorbed into the larger, served population groups as they deserve to be.

Patrons with Disabilities or Problem Patrons: Which Model Should Librarians Apply to People with Mental Illness?

Thomas E. Hecker

SUMMARY. While most treatments of library services to mentally ill patrons focus on them as problem patrons, a better model to follow for providing services on libraries is the disability model, based on the Americans with Disabilities Act (ADA). Using sources from psychological and sociological literature as well as library sources, the author presents a practical approach to the delivery of library and information services to mentally ill patrons with a measure of understanding and accommodation. *[Article copies available from The Haworth Document Delivery Service: 1-800-342-9678.]*

The phrase "problem patron," with its alliterative strength, is defined in the minds of librarians and library assistants by the sum

Thomas E. Hecker is Coordinator of Disabilities Services, University of Kentucky Libraries, Lexington, KY 40502.

[Haworth co-indexing entry note]: "Patrons with Disabilities or Problem Patrons: Which Model Should Librarians Apply to People with Mental Illness?" Hecker, Thomas E. Co-published simultaneously in *The Reference Librarian* (The Haworth Press, Inc.) No. 53, 1996, pp. 5-12; and: *Reference Services for the Unserved* (ed: Fay Zipkowitz) The Haworth Press, Inc., 1996, pp. 5-12. Single or multiple copies of this article are available from The Haworth Document Delivery Service: [1-800-342-9678, 9:00 a.m. - 5:00 p.m. (EST)].

of experiences they have had with difficult patrons, and also by the exchange of stories of experiences, which can comprise a folklore or history of difficult dealings in a particular library. Old-timers will coach newcomers in strategies to deal with difficult patrons, and in meetings groups will often identify difficult patrons and discuss strategies to manage them. More formally, many libraries have problem patron manuals and codes of behavior posted. A fair body of literature exists discussing different aspects of the problem patron issue. The most salient aspect of a patron labeled as a problem is his or her behavior, or rather misbehavior; problem patrons are those who violate the behavioral norms associated with libraries in particular or society in general. In libraries, people whose behavior offends are labeled, devalued, and reduced to "problem" status. This is what will hereafter be referred to as the problem patron model in dealing with difficult patrons. This article will challenge the use of the problem patron model in regard to patrons with mental illness, and develop an alternative and more constructive model, the disability model. People with mental illness are people with disabilities, who are explicitly covered by the Americans with Disabilities Act. A symptom or manifestation of mental illness is behavior which may offend or disturb people, just as a manifestation of paraplegia is the inability to use the legs, and just as blindness is associated with the an inability to sense light. Abnormal behavior is the defining external manifestation of mental illness as a disability.

Erving Goffman, a sociologist eminent for his study of mental patients and social interaction, wrote in *Behavior in Public Places: Notes on the Social Organization of Gatherings*:

> In diagnosing mental disorder and following its hospital course, psychiatrists typically cite aspects of the patient's behavior that are "inappropriate in the situation." Since this special kind of misconduct is believed to provide one obvious sign of "mental sickness," psychiatrists have given much time to these improprieties, developing the orientation and observational skills needed to study them . . .[1]

And again in Goffman's *Interaction Ritual: Essays on Face-to-Face Behavior*:

> I am suggesting, then, that symptomatic behavior might well be seen, in the first instance, not as a tortured form of two-person communication but as a form of social misconduct, in the sense that Emily Post and Amy Vanderbilt recognize this term.[2]

Behavior that is an object for diagnosis and study for psychiatrists–appropriate in a sense in a mental ward–can be inappropriate and disruptive in the library, where it is not of clinical interest but simply causes discomfort for workers or patrons. Those who offend against the social order may expect to be sanctioned in some way, the harshness of the sanctions depending on the severity of the offense. Persons committing minor offenses will suffer the frowns of people around them, perhaps verbal admonishments if the behavior is middling offensive, and on to legal sanctions for the most serious of offenses. These sanctions are levied in defense of the accepted social order, and are applied with as much moral assurance as Ann Landers' remonstrances in her syndicated column. We librarians may be reluctant to sanction people because of the social cost of creating a scene and because those we sanction lose face, to our sympathetic embarrassment, especially if the sanctioning is done publicly, but the problem patron model assists us in taking steps to maintain order in the library. The problem patron model lends our efforts–successful or not–at maintaining the social order moral assurance and moral weight. The patron is clearly cast as the problem to be manipulated and dealt with. We need not cast about for support in this stance–in our workplaces and in our professional literature we find many others who support sanctions, however regrettably, and who endorse the labeling of offenders as "problem patrons," a label such people may perhaps live down if their behavior comes to approximate accepted standards or a brand permanently affixed to those who will not, or who cannot, "shape up."

But can we always feel moral assurance when applying the problem patron model? The passage of the Americans with Disabilities Act of 1990 addressed the fact that people with disabilities have historically been discriminated against in our society, and that legislative relief was necessary for people with disabilities to have equal opportunity for employment and equal access to goods and services. Physical, sensory, mental, and emotional disabilities are all covered by the ADA. A mental impairment is defined by the ADA as: "any mental or psychological disorder, such as mental retardation, organic brain syndrome, emotional or mental illness, and specific learning disabilities."[3] Thus, mental illness is recognized by the law as a disability, with the same protections as other disabilities such as paraplegia, blindness, or hearing impairment.

The Americans with Disabilities Act mandates accommodations for people with disabilities so they can participate in employment and in all other aspects of society, including public places and public events. People who use wheelchairs are being accommodated with curb cuts in sidewalks, with designated parking areas, and with architectural changes to facilitate access to and use of buildings and other areas. People with hearing impairments are being provided with captioning and with special telecommunication services to accommodate their needs for communicating with others. People with visual impairments are being accommodated with materials in Braille or audio format, special equipment for magnification or scanning of texts, voice synthesis, and with human assistants for reading and transcribing. These accommodations are made recognizing the particular natures of each disability, and the changes needed to equalize access and opportunities as much as possible. But what must be done to accommodate people with mental illness in our society? Since abnormal behavior is the external manifestation of mental illness as a disability, accommodation for people with mental illness simply involves tolerance of behavior which does not approximate accepted norms. Now, I am not advocating unlimited tolerance of any and all behavior, because I believe our accepted norms for social interaction encourage productivity, health, and happiness for the greater part of our society, but I am suggesting that, in order to accommodate people with mental illness, tolerance of behavior "inappropriate in the situation" is necessary.

Of course librarians in many of our libraries are practicing this tolerance up to, and sometimes beyond, the breaking point. The accommodation involving tolerance I am suggesting is already, in many cases, being made and people with mental illness have access to libraries despite inappropriate behavior, so long as the behavior is not seriously antisocial or criminal. Libraries, especially large urban libraries, are taking the brunt of what Dr. E. Fuller Torrey calls "The Scandalous Neglect of the Mentally Ill Homeless."[4] Because of the fiasco of the public policy of deinstitutionalizing the seriously mentally ill, with insufficient community resources to support them as well as an unwelcoming public, libraries are serving as homeless shelters and as surrogate parts of the mental health system. This is a burden librarians and their institutions ought not to bear. As Leonard Kniffel of the Detroit Public Library wrote:

> Some of them could clear a room with their odor, but as long as they obeyed the rules, we respected their right to be in the library, even though there were days when I'd gaze across the reference room and swear I was an attendant in an insane asylum.[5]

This is a sorry state of affairs for our libraries, and certainly not a state I endorse. Yet the tragedy is not so much with the state of our libraries as it is a tragedy for the mentally ill homeless who need social services and social support. The only solution for this tragedy is for American society to develop a will to provide for its own citizens, with equal insurance coverage and with improved medical and social services.

Besides the glaring plight of the mentally ill homeless, who are essentially outcasts from society, there are millions of people who have mental illness, or who have had mental illness, who have assimilated back into society to a greater or lesser degree, depending upon the severity of the illness and the efficacy of the treatment they received. People with mental illness covered by the Americans with Disabilities Act cover the gamut, from those who have completely recovered (called "the mentally restored") who usually pass as not having undergone treatment, a strategy used to avoid stigmatization, rejection, and discrimination, to those with mild and controllable symptoms, to those with troublesome symptoms, to those with intractable symptoms. People with mental illness may be our parents, our siblings, our spouses, our children, our colleagues, or ourselves. The mentally ill homeless, one third of the homeless population, are simply the most visible and most remarked upon segment of the population of people with mental illness.[6] When I suggest that librarians ought to apply the disability model to people with mental illness, I do not mean that we should apply the model to people who are spectacularly in need of social services and medical treatment. Using the medical model, such people are akin to people who are in the throes of a heart attack, or people with pneumonia, who ought to receive immediate attention: in the case of acute mental illness such people do not receive medical attention because of a variety of legal, political, and social reasons other authors have enumerated. Rather, I suggest that librarians apply the disability model to patrons with mental illness who have retained, or who have regained, a level of functioning which is still within the pale of society. Such people may exhibit symptoms which "stretch the envelope" of our tolerance, but if tolerance will allow them to live an acceptable life within society, tolerance is the accommodation which must be accorded them.

The application of different viewpoints, or models as social scientists put it, can have profound effects on the way people are treated. In ancient and medieval times a religious model was often applied to mental illness, which held the illness was divine punishment or that people with mental illness were inhabited by demons or were victims of witchcraft.[7] Later came the medical model, which recognized that mental illnesses were indeed illnesses, although only recently has research shown that mental illnesses are organic conditions originating in the physical structure of the brain. Mental illnesses are no-fault brain diseases; just as any organ of the body is subject to malfunction, so is the brain. For a long time the medical model was supported by psychological functionalism, which did not know of the cause of the illnesses but worked backward from the effect, the symptoms, and posited an illness.[8] Now organic causes have been found. The medical model led to the human treatment of people with mental illness, and since the biochemical revolution of the 1960s has led to much more effective medical treatment of mental illness.

Today, since the Americans with Disabilities Act has taken effect, mental illness may be viewed from a new perspective, the disability model. Rather than applying the label of problem patron to persons with mental illness, librarians must recognize people with mental illness as people with disabilities who ought to receive a measure of understanding and accommodation. A question arises: how can people with a mental disability be discerned? Unlike paraplegia or other disabilities with recognizable external signs, mental disability is an invisible or hidden disability. Although librarians will perform amateur diagnoses on occasion to cope with situations, most librarians lack the credentials to make credible diagnoses. This is better left to physicians and psychiatrists, although there can be professional differences of opinion in the difficult area of diagnosing mental illness. Perhaps it is best for librarians to work under assumptions made in their best judgment, or to work under no assumptions at all. A person, for whatever reason, whose behavior deviates from accepted standards ought to be tolerated as far as possible to allow them the benefits of society. Such people have a behavioral impairment just as some people have a visual impairment or a hearing impairment. People with behavioral impairments ought to be reasonably accommodated just as people with other impairments, medically certified or not. Many people have disabilities which have not been formally diagnosed or certified, so it may be best to work from prima facie evidence.

Rather than the moral assurance we have when applying the problem patron model to someone who has offended against the social order in our libraries, librarians ought to apply the disability model and realize that people with disabilities, including people with mental illness, have a moral (and now legal) claim on us for understanding and accommodation. The moral assurance is actually on the side of the person with a disability, who has the right to reject the label of "problem patron" as patronizing and judgmental. Do we have the right to apply such a label?

REFERENCES

1. Erving Goffman, *Behavior in Public Places; Notes on the Social Organization of Gatherings*, (New York: Free Press of Glencoe, 1963), 3.

2. Erving Goffman, "Mental Symptoms and Public Order" in *Interaction Ritual: Essays on Face-to-Face Behavior*, (New York: Pantheon, 1967), 140.

3. Equal Employment Opportunity Commission, *Technical Assistance Manual for the Americans With Disabilities Act*, (Warren Gorham Lamont), II-2.

4. E. Fuller Torrey, "Thirty Years of Shame: the Scandalous Neglect of the Mentally Ill Homeless," *National Forum* 73 (Winter 1993): 4.

5. Leonard Kniffel, "Food, Treatment–not Access–are Solutions,"*American Libraries* 22 (March 1991): 188.

6. Torrey, "Thirty Years of Shame: the Scandalous Neglect of the Mentally Ill Homeless," 4.

7. R. D. Milns, "Squibb Academic Lecture: Attitudes Toward Mental Illness in Antiquity," *Australian and New Zealand Journal of Psychiatry* 20 (1986) 454-462.

8. Erving Goffman, "The Medical Model and Mental Hospitalization" in *Asylums: Essays on the Social Situation of Mental Patients and Other Inmates*, (Garden City, New York: Anchor, 1961), 350.

Library Services to Disabled Students: Outreach and Education

Katy Lenn

SUMMARY. With the passage of the American with Disabilities Act (ADA) academic institutions have worked to accommodate students who seek access to their programs. Libraries, too, must develop ways to meet the needs of disabled college and university students. This article discusses some approaches to meeting those needs. *[Article copies available from The Haworth Document Delivery Service: 1-800-342-9678.]*

Congress acknowledged that society's accumulated myths and fear about disability and disease are as handicapping as are the physical limitations that flow from actual impairment.

–Warren Burger,
Associate Justice, Supreme Court

It is often said that the easiest minority to join is the disabled. "Each year there are 500,000 new head injuries, 15,000 new amputees, 10,000 new spinal injury cases, and 500,000 strokes. A total of up to 500,000 people have multiple sclerosis, and 200,000 have AIDS. Each of these conditions results in severe physical disability" (United States, 1992). Add to this an estimated 1.8 million with

---

Katy Lenn is Reference Librarian, Knight Library of Oregon, Eugene, OR 97403-1299.

[Haworth co-indexing entry note]: "Library Services to Disabled Students: Outreach and Education." Lenn, Katy. Co-published simultaneously in *The Reference Librarian* (The Haworth Press, Inc.) No. 53, 1996, pp. 13-25; and: *Reference Services for the Unserved* (ed: Fay Zipkowitz) The Haworth Press, Inc., 1996, pp. 13-25. Single or multiple copies of this article are available from The Haworth Document Delivery Service: [1-800-342-9678, 9:00 a.m. - 5:00 p.m. (EST)].

13

learning disabilities, 6.5 million with mental retardation and 39.9 million with some type of mental disorder and you have the equivalent of the entire population of two states, California and Texas. As the United States' population continues to age this number is expected to rise significantly. Putting this in another perspective, Hispanics represent 9 percent of the population and Blacks 12 percent, but 17 percent of the U.S. population is disabled. Yet this sizable population has largely been ignored, usually for the reasons so aptly stated by Justice Burger above.

Although myths and fears associated with disabilities are subsiding, years of unfair treatment and apathy have presented challenges beyond those created by the disability. Legislation has been enacted to rectify the situation and put the disabled on equal footing with the rest of society. The 1991 Americans with Disabilities Act (ADA), brought the needs and the rights of the disabled to the national forefront. This legislation creates the impetus for change through fear of lawsuit but organizations should thrust themselves into the spirit of the law and strive to be proactive.

It is important to remember that the purpose of legislation for the disabled is not to create special rights but equal rights. In fact, the ADA specifically states that organizations must provide the most integrated setting possible for people with disabilities. The ADA seeks to rectify the isolating conditions experienced by people with disabilities. While it may not appear that society has isolated the disabled, one only needs to look at a 1986 Louis Harris and Associates poll of people with disabilities to discover otherwise. It found that "17 percent of people with disabilities never eat in restaurants compared to 5 percent of nondisabled people . . . Thirteen percent of people with disabilities say they never go to a grocery store compared with only 2 percent of the rest of the population" (United States, 1989). The disabled should be woven in to the fabric of society to be an integral part not just an accessory.

It is important to remember that the library needs of people with disabilities are no different from those of any other patron. The only difference may be in the way the library and information are accessed, requiring a shift in the traditional methods. Given the rapid change in libraries, shifts to accommodate people with disabilities should be viewed as just another change.

Libraries, due to the nature of the materials they house and the age of the buildings they reside in, have traditionally been formidable places for people with disabilities. It is often a Catch-22 when it comes to making improvements. If a building/service is inhospitable, people will most likely stop using it. When individuals stop using a service, they often stop providing input, and without input, changes are rarely made. Libraries must be proactive, working to gather input and make changes. After all, "If you build it they will come."

TYPES OF DISABILITIES

There are many types of people, and many types of disabilities. The needs of people vary from person to person and disability to disability. This section will touch on a few disabilities and the ways they manifest themselves. As this is not a treatise on disabilities, the discussion will be done only in most general of terms. Some disabilities are more visible than others; and even if a disability is apparent, a person's needs may not be. One should never assume by merely looking at someone what their needs may be.

For some with invisible disabilities it can be difficult to ask for help because it may mean disclosing their disability. Since the change in society's attitudes is occurring at glacier speed, it is not unusual for individuals to be apprehensive about disclosing their disability and risk being labelled or ridiculed. Imagine having to expose a personal secret to every individual you ask for assistance and doing this on an almost daily basis, and you can better understand their trepidation.

Visual impairments include a wide range of visual abilities, ranging from some perception or restricted visual fields to no light perception. Some individuals may use enlargement or special glasses to read. Some may need the assistance of a cane or guide dog and some may not use a device at all.

There are many reasons for mobility impairments and the outcomes are equally as varied. The most obvious example are people that use a wheelchair or other mobility aid such as crutches. But there are others that because of pulmonary, respiratory or other ailments may walk without aid, but may find long distances, stairs or other physical demands difficult. Some may have an upper extremity impairment that may affect ability to write or manipulate objects.

Hearing impairments include a wide range of hearing loss from hard of hearing to profound deafness. Some people hear high tones, others low tones. Loss may be experienced in one or both ears. Some people will rely on hearing aids, some will read lips, and others will use sign language or oral interpreters. Some people may use a combination of various methods but is incorrect to assume that ALL hearing impaired people use one method. Some individuals may choose to speak, others may not. Hearing aids can improve hearing but in most cases do not restore it completely. Shouting does not improve comprehension.

Some individuals experience difficulties receiving, storing, processing, remembering, or transmitting information in one or more formats (written, oral or kinesthetic). These are some of the effects of learning disabilities. Individuals may find that it affects their concentration or attention to detail. While this is not a new area, it has received wider attention over the last ten years. This group of patrons can be all but invisible to staff.

There are many other disabilities. Some include speech/communication, mental retardation, and mental illness. All present different needs.

OBSTACLES FOUND IN A LIBRARY

The following section identifies problem areas in libraries for patrons with disabilities and the nature of these difficulties.

Poor *communication* creates one of the worst hinderances for library patrons, and can leave a long-lasting impression. Many services in library settings are accomplished through personal interaction and signage. Initial contact with staff is usually at a service desk. The desk itself can create a communication obstacle. High desks, designed without lower sections, create barriers for people in wheelchairs. Library literature is replete with articles discussing the need for equal eye contact with patrons. Imagine the frustration of encountering a high desk in a wheelchair; being unable to adjust your height to talk to library staff, then having to crane your neck from a sitting position to ask a question.

In addition to the physical surroundings, staff may feel uncomfortable talking to people with disabilities. This is usually caused by uncertainty about how to talk to people with disabilities. This uncomfortable/uncertain reaction can result in negative feelings, incomplete service, or incorrect answers.

Many patrons, disabled or not, are shy about asking for assistance or just like to work independently. Signage should strive to make self-sufficiency possible. Signs that are not clearly printed or not available in Braille make it difficult for people with visual impairments. Maps and shelf labels are notorious for being confusing to patrons; add to this equation a learning disability and it escalates from frustrating to antagonistic.

While the difficulties that *print materials* present those with visual impairments is obvious, there is another segment of library patrons that have difficulty with print–those with learning disabilities. While able to see words, some with learning disabilities may have difficulty reading the words.

Other items collected by libraries that can be difficult for patrons with disabilities are *non-print materials*. Non-captioned videos can be difficult, if not useless, for hearing impaired individuals. If patrons use interpreters for uncaptioned videos it becomes difficult to watch the video and interpreter at the same time.

Computer based materials have changed the way business is conducted in libraries. There are few reference areas left that do not use at least one computer system. From in-house catalogs to CD-ROMs to Internet, the computer has revolutionized libraries.

Interacting with computers can be difficult for people with visual impairments and learning disabilities. To the extent that computer programs use sound (beeps, music, or spoken words) to convey information, people with hearing impairments may also have difficulties. For individuals without fine motor movements, using a keyboard or mouse may be impossible.

As the use of computer format for information delivery evolves, it presents both wonderful opportunities and increased frustration for those with disabilities. The Graphical User Interfaces (GUI's), such as Windows, that make navigating screens easier for those with sight, create an additional hurdle for those without sight.

Physical access issues are some of the most common and obvious

barriers encountered by patrons. These range from the ramp into the building to restrooms stalls. There are also the more subtle obstacles. Tables may appear high enough but with the addition of an apron, do not provide enough clearance for someone in a wheelchair. Restrooms may be equipped with an accessible stall, but do not have accessible sinks or towel dispensers. Spaces may be inadequate for wheelchairs to back up, open a door, or turn around. Lack of handrails could mean potential falls for individuals with balance, mobility, or visual problems. Life-threatening obstacles include emergency alarms that cannot be seen by the hard of hearing.

This is only a thumbnail sketch of potential obstacles. While there are similarities among libraries, each library has its own set of obstacles. It is important to determine what obstacles may be particular to each library.

REMEDIES

Most obstacles can be eliminated or easily minimized. It is important to remember that some remedies may come easily but that some may take time; some will require little effort and money but others may require more.

The following suggestions are meant as a catalyst to help libraries produce their own remedies. There is no comprehensive list of remedies or quick-fixes.

To ensure that a library's efforts are organized and planned properly, libraries should appoint one person to serve as coordinator. This need not be a full time position, but it must be understood that this position will require extra time and effort, and should be taken into consideration when assigning the position. Assigning this responsibility to someone who is already overburdened will affect the person and the service. Financial compensation may also be required based on existing responsibilities.

A coordinator's responsibility is to be familiar with the needs of the disabled and the various remedies available. This means being aware of possibilities that not every product, make, and model are on the market. There are places to receive input. This means going beyond the library walls to the city/town and/or university community.

The coordinator should recommend policies and procedures and oversee staff training. While it is the coordinator's responsibility to direct the efforts of the library, it does not exonerate the rest of the staff from providing quality service to patrons with disabilities.

Establishing what remedies are needed begins with determining what needs exist. Talking to patrons and non-patrons alike will help establish a list of items that cause difficulty for people with disabilities. Reaching out to patrons may require establishing strong contacts with the office on campus that works with students with disabilities or groups in the community. These contacts will not only provide insight but suggestions for specific remedies.

Surveys can be effective but generally receive rather low response rates with this population. These low response rates may not justify the time spent creating the questionnaire. Direct contact with people will most likely produce better results. One-on-one interviews are a very good method but the drawback to this method is that it can be time-consuming. Attending meetings of local advocacy groups, adding the library to the agenda, and asking for recommendations can also be worthwhile.

Another way to achieve direct contact is through focus groups. The University of Oregon Library recently conducted a focus group session with several students with disabilities and found this arrangement beneficial for several reasons. Most of the students had not met before, but because every participant had a disability, there was no apprehension about speaking about their disabilities. Some found that others are confronting the same difficulties in university life; a reassuring thought. The format provided an excellent forum for receiving feedback on library services. During the course of the session, students also shared ideas with each other; informing each other of services or equipment.

Contacts in the Library community will also provide information. There are materials on the ADA (Foos, Green), service (Lenn, McNulty, Vellman) and technology (Jones, Kneedler, Lazzaro, Mates). There are several electronic bulletin boards that can also provide practical information and insight into the needs of the disabled.

As *communication* is often the first contact patrons have with the Library, it should be the first area to receive attention. Staff should be trained how to communicate effectively with all patrons, along with disability etiquette. This should alleviate the discomfort staff may experience in unfamiliar situations. Part of their training should be reassuring them that it is acceptable to offer assistance.

Offering assistance should become a regular part of staff response. For instance, when a page indicates where a book can be found, a typical response may be "Around the corner and to your left." Add to the end of this response "Would you like me to show you?" and the door has been opened to the patron, such as those with learning disabilities, who find the stacks confusing. They do not have to expose themselves by admitting that the directions "around the corner and to the left" may be useless. This not only helps the patron but provides excellent public relations opportunities. As staff become more comfortable serving patrons with disabilities, they may become one of the best sources for information on obstacles and remedies.

Since everything from book renewals to reference questions take place over the telephone, libraries should have a TDD (telephone communication device for the deaf). TDD's allow people with hearing impairments to communicate by phone. There are other methods, such as using a relay system (operator acts as interpreter between TDD and a regular phone) to place calls, but a TDD allows for more independence and privacy. While not every service desk needs to be equipped with a TDD, there should be at least one in the library. Staff should be trained and if the TDD is not used often, should have regularly retraining. A policy to handle TDD calls that cannot be answered by the receiving desk should be in place. As TDD calls cannot be transferred to regular phones, a message system should be established to ensure that requests are forwarded and answered, via TDD, with the same speed of all phone inquires. The TDD number should be advertised in all library publications, phone books, and directories geared toward the hearing impaired. Patrons derive a great deal of information about the library through signage. Signage can be both a help and a hinderance. Good signage allows patrons to work independently; poor signage frustrates users and wastes time. As mentioned previously, providing inadequate or poor signage can force some individuals, who may prefer to work on their own, to reveal their disability and ask for help. Throughout the library, signs should be easy to read and understand. Lettering should be kept simple and with bold and contrasting colors. International access symbols and Braille should be used whenever appropriate. Shelving labels with call numbers should be clearly marked with bold lettering, and placed so low vision patrons can get up close to read them.

To set the tone for the library, a sign at the entrance that states "If you have a disability and would like assistance, please advise staff" is suggested. This sign automatically creates an atmosphere of acceptance and a willingness to serve.

Libraries generally deal with two types of *print material:* library generated material and material acquired by the library. Obviously, library generated material is easier to manipulate. Library handouts that are generated by computer can be produced in large-print at a relatively low cost. While the benefits of large print for the visually impaired are obvious, there are some people with learning disabilities that experience an increase in comprehension with larger text. Adjusting font size will require reformatting and will likely increase the number of pages, but should not require an enormous investment of time or money.

Keeping copies of handouts on disk creates not only an easy method for updating, but a disk could be a patrons preferred format. Patrons that have computers that enlarge text or synthesize data may find this helpful. Transferring material to Braille may be costly and something that the library may not be able to do in-house. Arrangements can be made with a community group or office on campus to provide Braille copies on an as-needed basis. Some materials, such as tours, are excellent candidates for tape recording.

Accessibility becomes more complicated when dealing with materials acquired by the library. Large print versions are available. These books, however, tend to be popular titles that serve public libraries well but are generally not acquired by academic libraries. Books-on-tape fall in this same popular-title category. Braille versions of books are difficult to find and may not be the best solution to serve the widest audience. The coordinator should be aware of alternatives for patron access to these materials. National and state talking book and Braille services often serve any individual that has extreme difficulty reading standard text.

Acquiring material on disk or online is another option. The number of available titles is growing. Items on the Internet, e.g., through Project Gutenberg, are a great boon to those using computers to access text.

The remaining option is for libraries to purchase regular formats and create accessibility after materials are received. The most general remedy is to enlarge the print. There are several methods available for enlargement. For instance, the enlarging capabilities of a photocopy machine are often overlooked. While this is not the method of choice for an entire book, it does provide a simple and fast method for producing a passage in large type.

A closed circuit television (CCTV), involving a camera and a screen, is another method for enlarging text. One advantage of the CCTVs are that they can enlarge handwritten text and newspapers as well as standard book text. Like all equipment they range in features and costs. Some work with standard televisions, others have their own screen; some use stationary cameras, some use handheld models; some interact with computers and some enlarge computer text. Since each feature is important for different reasons, several elements should be considered: (1) patron needs; (2) cost and budget limitations; (3) system use, compatibility (stand-alone or part of a larger system), upgrading possibilities; and (4) training and staffing needs.

Beyond CCTVs the technological innovations are astounding. There are software programs that enlarge computer text and use voice synthesizers to read text aloud. At the more sophisticated end are systems, such as the Kurzweill, designed to scan and synthesize text and voice recognition software. The availability of different systems has grown and the decline in cost makes them more of a reality for libraries.

As this equipment is still expensive and not always easy to use, training, placement, security and staffing are all issues that must be considered along with the cost of the system.

Because funding usually poses a problem, consider joint use. For example, many offices, such as Special Collections, would also like to have use of a scanner. Splitting the cost could make it more viable for both parties. A clear understanding of time and schedule must be established so neither the patron or the other department are left out.

There are several methods for creating accessible *non-print materials* for the hearing impaired. Closed captioning is one of the most common methods. Closed captioning displays dialogue on the screen but it only appears after being decoded. A library's policy should be to buy closed-captioned videos whenever available. Videos of most current major films are available, but older titles and educational films are not always readily available.

If a library provides viewing for its patrons, equipment should be able to decode captioned films. All newer television sets (as of June 1993) are able to read closed captioning. Older sets may require a decoding box. For those with hearing impairments, small amplification systems can be used in conjunction with the television.

If closed captioning is not available the options become more complicated. Software is available to create open captioned versions of videos. Opened captioned films have captioning visible at all times. Creating open captioned films requires certain equipment (decocder, computer, etc.) and time. Time may be the biggest investment since the script must be typed on a word processor. Copyright restrictions must also be followed.

There are companies that create closed captioned versions of videos. Considerable expense is involved and this may not be a viable option.

The United States Department of Education supports a free loan program for persons and organizations serving the hearing impaired. Open captioned versions of both educational and popular films are available. There could be some delay, so requests should be made well in advance of showing. The address and phone number of this service appears at the end of this article.

For people with visual impairments, video needs are quite different. A new service, Descriptive Video Service (DVS) "provides narrated descriptions of a program or movie's key visual elements without interfering with the program dialogue. The narration describes elements such as actions, body language, settings, graphics and subtitles" (Descriptive Video Service, 1994). DVS is available for some public television programming. DVS programs are broadcast free to viewers by a number of public television stations nationwide. The service can be accessed with the Second Audio Program (S.A.P.) features on stereo televisions or VCRs, or with a decoder. The address and phone number of DVS is available at the end of this article.

As noted earlier, *computer based systems* have changed the way libraries operate. Many reference materials preferred by patrons involve computers. These computers create incredible opportunities and new challenges. For print-impaired users much of this information was inaccessible prior to the advent of the computer. Text that could not be read, can now be enlarged, synthesized, or printed in Braille. There is no dearth of adaptive computer equipment. The best advice is to contact experts who can provide information and insight into the adaptive technology maze.

When dealing with *physical access*, the first step should be to take stock of the surroundings. Assess how many of the tables are wheelchair accessible; whether vending machines, copy machines, water fountains and other devices are at appropriate heights. Ask community groups to go through the library, making suggestions for improvements. To receive a wide range of suggestions, invite people with a variety of disabilities.

In situations where access cannot be accomplished–in libraries this is often the stacks–be prepared to provide patrons with an alternative, such as a retrieval service. For individuals that may find it difficult to make trips to the library, offer a proxy service. A proxy service maintains their responsibility for the items checked out but relieves them of the burden of having to retrieve material. Consider offering the in-house loan of a book truck for an individual who cannot carry books.

CONCLUSION

There are obstacles to patrons with disabilities but there are also solutions. This article has tried to demonstrate that making libraries more accessible and eliminating obstacles is not a formidable task. The huge number of people with disabilities, the obvious moral and legal obligations, and the ease of implementing accommodations all provide reasons for changing libraries. One additional reason–we are making these changes for ourselves. After all, the disabled population is the easiest minority to join; an accident today and you could be a part of this minority tomorrow.

REFERENCES

Association of Research Libraries. Office of Management Services. (1991). *Library services for persons with disabilities*. Washington, DC: Association of Research Libraries, Spec Kit 176.

Descriptive Video Service. (1994). *DVS Guide, 5*, p(1).

Foos, D. and Pack, N., (Eds.) (1992) *How libraries must comply with the Americans with Disabilities Act*. Phoenix: Oryx.

Green, M. (1993). Implementing the Americans with Disabilities Act: A bibliography for academic libraries. *Texas Library Journal, 69*, 99-102.

Jones, R. (1993). Adaptive computer technology: An overview. *Library Hi Tech, 11*, 30-33.

Kneedler, W. & Sizemore, E.J. (1993). Speech synthesis + online library catalog + "talking catalog" *Library Hi Tech, 11*, 57-65.

Lazzaro, J. (1993). *Adaptive technologies for learning and work environments*. Chicago: American Library Association.

Lenn, K. (1993). Climbing the mountain: The Americans with Disabilities Act and libraries. *Wilson Library Bulletin, 68*, 36-39.

Mates, B. (1993). Adaptive technology for the 90's. *Computers in Libraries, 13*, 54-5.

McNulty, T. (1993). *Access to information: materials, technologies, and services for print impaired readers*. Chicago: American Library Association.

Project EASI (1993). *Project EASI's adaptive computing evaluation kit for colleges and universities*. Washington, DC: Interuniversity Communications Council.

United States. Senate. Committee on Labor and Human Resources. (1989). *Americans with Disabilities Act of 1989: Hearings before the Committee on Labor and Human Resources and the Subcommittee on the handicapped*. Washington, DC: GPO, 1989.

United States. House. Committee on Appropriations. (1992). *Departments of Labor, Health and Human Services, Education and Related Agencies appropriations for 1993: Hearings before a subcommittee of the Committee on Appropriations*. Washington: GPO.

Velleman, R. (1990). *Meeting the needs of people with disabilities*. Phoenix: Oryx.

VIDEOS

Descriptive Video Service WGBH, 125 Western Ave., Boston, MA 02134.

Captioned Films/Video, Modern Talking Picture Service, Inc., 5000 Park St. North, St. Petersburg, FL 33709.

Meeting the Information Needs of Battered Women: Responsibilities and Roles for Library and Information Science

Patricia Dewdney
Roma M. Harris
Christina Lockerby

SUMMARY. Wife assault is an important social problem that needs to be addressed by librarians and library and information science (LIS) researchers concerned with the way in which battered women search for information. This paper reports on two studies in which the social service network is viewed as a type of information system and which question the effectiveness of community responses to the information needs of battered women. The results of these studies suggest several ways in which LIS professionals can better assist three client groups: individual battered women, social service providers, and public policy or decision makers. *[Article copies available from The Haworth Document Delivery Service: 1-800-342-9678.]*

Patricia Dewdney and Roma M. Harris are on the faculty of the Graduate School of Library and Information Science, University of Western Ontario, London, Ontario, Canada N6G 1H1. Christina Lockerby is an MLIS student. Correspondence should be sent to the first author.

Part of the research for this article was done with the financial support of the Social Sciences and Humanities Research Council of Canada, Grant #410-89-0227.

[Haworth co-indexing entry note]: "Meeting the Information Needs of Battered Women: Responsibilities and Roles for Library and Information Science." Dewdney, Patricia, Roma M. Harris, and Christina Lockerby. Co-published simultaneously in *The Reference Librarian* (The Haworth Press, Inc.) No. 53, 1996, pp. 27-45; and: *Reference Services for the Unserved* (ed: Fay Zipkowitz) The Haworth Press, Inc., 1996, pp. 27-45. Single or multiple copies of this article are available from The Haworth Document Delivery Service: [1-800-342-9678, 9:00 a.m. - 5:00 p.m. (EST)].

INTRODUCTION

Wife assault or woman abuse are terms commonly used to describe the physical or psychological abuse directed by a man against his female partner in order to intimidate and control her. Conservative estimates suggest that approximately one woman in eight encounters violence at the hands of her male partner, and some studies put the incidence as high as 50 to 60% of all women who have male partners (see, e.g., Walker, 1984; MacLeod, 1989.) Wife assault knows no demographic limits: it occurs in all strata of society, among people who are diverse in terms of age, occupation, race, ethnicity, and education, although violence in more affluent groups tends to be less visible because these women use emergency shelters and community legal clinics less often than others (Greaves, Heapy and Wylie, 1988, p. 41).

Women may stay in abusive relationships for many reasons including financial dependence, low self-esteem, and the threat of further violence. However, since information-seeking can be a useful coping response for managing stressful situations (Lazarus & Folkman, 1990), it is not surprising that many battered women eventually seek help and information beyond their own internal resources as they attempt to ameliorate their situations or distance themselves from their violent partners. Research on citizen information-seeking suggests that most people in need of coping information tend to use interpersonal sources such as family and friends in preference to formal institutions (see, e.g., Chen & Hernon, 1982; Beal, 1979). While the same is true for battered women, the information-seeking process may be more problematic for assaulted women than it is for other citizens. Family and friends may not always be trustworthy sources of help; indeed, access to interpersonal support systems of any kind may be difficult simply because women are often deliberately isolated from others by their abusive partners. In other words, the nature of the problem faced by battered women often prevents them from reaching the types of help which are physically and psychologically accessible to most other people. Perhaps for this reason it has been suggested that battered women often have very little idea of the community resources available to them (Homer, Leonard and Taylor, 1985).

Battered women also face the usual barriers inherent in the social service networks of any community. In fact, Levinson (1988) suggests that while not knowing where to turn for help is the single biggest problem for all citizens; even once a potential source of help is located further barriers exist due to bureaucratic processes, restricted admissions and extended waiting lists (this is particularly true for emergency housing), discriminatory practices, poor service quality, inconvenient hours, long travel distances, lack of accessible transportation or child care, and language or cultural barriers (pp. 3-4).

In most communities, dealing with the problem of "where to turn for help," i.e., the provision of community information and referral, is the *primary* mandate of two organizations–public libraries and community information centers.[1] However, nearly all agencies that comprise the social service network have at least a partial information and referral function, and thus can be viewed as nodes within a much larger information service network or system. Indeed, instead of turning to libraries or I & R centers, citizens of all kinds routinely turn to government agencies, physicians, the police and social workers for information that will help them define their options or understand the scope of the problem situations they face before making decisions about the actions they need to take or the kinds of help they want.

In many situations, service providers or agencies are contacted for referrals simply because they are perceived to be familiar, accessible sources of help. This approach to help-seeking may not always produce optimal results, however, particularly for assaulted women. If such familiarity leads a woman to contact a clergy member or family physician, for example, she may encounter a person who is not trained to assess multi-faceted problems, who is unfamiliar with appropriate referral procedures, and who may be unaware of the range of possible services available in the community. For example, Trute, Sarsfield and MacKenzie (1988, p. 62) reported that battered women are rarely referred by physicians to other sources of help in the community.

For LIS professionals who are interested in facilitating an improved information system for assaulted women and service providers, a summary is provided in the next section of this paper of two studies in which the problem of wife assault has been analyzed from an information-seeking perspective.

THE INFORMATION NEEDS OF BATTERED WOMEN

Although some studies in social science have mapped the process of help-seeking by women who have been assaulted by their male partners, a study by Harris (1988) represents the first attempt to create a typology of the information needs of battered women, where information needs were modelled theoretically as "knowledge gaps." Interviews with forty former residents of a shelter for battered women revealed two general categories of information needs: (1) a need for information about community resources and (2) a need for information that would help women understand themselves and their partners' roles in violent relationships. The needs most frequently identified in the study involved information about what to do during or immediately following a violent incident and how to manage in the future (p. 64). Consistent with the literature on general information-seeking, the most frequently used sources of information relied upon by this sample of assaulted women were their friends and family members. However, it is interesting to note that 30% of the respondents relied on reading material to answer their questions (although none mentioned libraries as a source of information or help).

COMMUNITY INFORMATION NEEDS:
THE CASE OF WIFE ASSAULT

Although Harris's study appears to be the only one that has directly addressed the information needs of battered women, it was restricted to responses from women who had already been at least partially successful in getting help with their situations. The study raises questions, then, as to how a more representative sample of women might go about seeking information to get help with the problem of wife assault and the degree of success they would have in reaching appropriate community agencies. To address these questions, Harris and Dewdney (1991) designed an extensive two-phase study in order to map the degree of overlap between the need for information about wife assault and the response offered through social service networks.

Methodology

The investigation focused on six communities, four of which were located in rural areas and two large urban centers. All six communities had police services, a hospital, and a public library. Of the four small communities, two did not have a women's shelter, and two had no generic community information (I & R) center. In the first part of the study, 543 randomly selected women were interviewed in a household survey to find out the kinds of community resources they thought would be helpful in a hypothetical situation in which a neighbor asked for help because she had been assaulted by her male partner. In phase two of the investigation, 163 telephone interviews were conducted with agencies and human service professionals identified during the household interviews as likely sources of different types of help, including information and referral. Agency respondents were asked to describe how their organization would typically handle requests for help from abused women (including intake procedures and referrals). In cases where the household respondents named professionals in private practice such as family physicians, lawyers or clergy members, individual professionals randomly selected from the telephone directory were asked to describe what would likely happen if a woman telephoned with a request for help of a particular kind.

Results

The detailed results of this study are described in *Library and Information Science Research*, *14*(1992), 5-29. Here, it is sufficient to review a few of the general results before focusing on their implications for information professionals.

The women interviewed during the household survey were familiar with the problem of wife assault. In fact, 60% indicated that they knew someone who had been abused by her partner and nearly 30% reported that they had been approached for help by an abused woman. The types of help most commonly perceived by the respondents to be necessary were a place to stay (70%), emotional support (51.2%), and professional counseling (38.3%). The sources of help most frequently named were women's shelters (60%), friends (50.5%), and police (42.9%).

Although many of the women's responses were predictable, such as linking the need for emergency housing with women's shelters, there were some surprising results. For instance, many of those who mentioned the need for emotional support named the police, lawyers and physicians as possible sources of such support. Data from other research on the actual responses of service providers indicates that such expectations on the part of the public may lead to considerable disappointment and conflict. Many police officers, for example, consider the provision of emotional support or counseling to be peripheral to their role (see, for example, Johnson, 1985). Furthermore, abused women frequently report that police officers minimize the severity of the violence they have experienced and/or behave in a judgmental, non-supportive fashion toward them (see, for example, Harris, 1988).

Our findings suggest that many women expect to find types of help in their communities which the service providers in those communities do not, in fact, provide. As well, it appears that some human service providers not only are unaware of appropriate sources of help for abused women and, thus, unable to make effective referrals, but they also fail to routinely assess the kind of help being sought. In other words, a woman who makes contact with the human services network and identifies herself as having experienced abuse may not necessarily be questioned about her immediate physical safety, nor is she guaranteed that the staff member who screens her request for help will even try to find out what kind of assistance she is seeking. This is particularly true in the case of professionals in practice who work independently of other community agencies, such as lawyers, physicians and members of the clergy.

Information and Referral

One result of this research that should be of special concern to LIS professionals is the way in which the term "information" was used by the women who were interviewed. For instance, the terms "community information" and "information and referral" seemed to have no special meaning for these respondents. In fact, they used the term "information about X" interchangeably with the term "help for X," supporting Dervin's (1983) view of information as that which helps people progress through a situation. "Getting information" was construed by respondents as "knowing about rights and options," for example, or "helping a woman decide on a course of action."

Although public libraries exist in all six communities studied and community information centers are located in four, of the 42 women (7.7% of study respondents) who used the terms "information" and/or "referral" when they were asked about the kind of help a battered woman might need, only one mentioned a community information (I & R) center and none mentioned a library in response to the question, "Where in [this community] would you call to get information and referral?" Clearly, then, despite their information mandates, these organizations lacked any meaningful profile as organizations that can provide coping or social service information. In contrast, agencies and service providers such as the Salvation Army, hospitals, social workers and welfare offices were often cited as the best sources of community information and referral services (see Table 1). This perception suggests that organizations which have I & R as their primary mandate should work much more closely with other types of community agencies if they are to be at all effective in a social services information advocacy role.

Use of the Telephone Directory

During the household interviews the women were asked in connection with the particular types of help they mentioned, "Where would you look in the phone book?" In response to this question they identified 172 different phone book headings. With the exception of the local emergency number (e.g., 911) which most respondents said they would call for physical protection or emergency housing, many women reported using terms such as "social or community services," "abuse" or "abused or battered wives" or "battered women" as access terms for trying to locate the names of potentially helpful agencies in the white, yellow or blue (government listings) pages of the phone book. Unfortunately, at the time of the survey, few listings could be located using these terms. Phone list-

TABLE 1. Sources Believed by Household Respondents to Provide Information and Referral

Source	Percent*
Salvation Army	35
Hospital	33
Social worker, welfare	31
Police	30
Church	22
Friend	20
Women's shelter	17
Family	5

* The total number of individual respondents was 42. The total percentage exceeds 100 because some respondents gave multiple responses.

ings in communities with women's shelters usually included them by name only, thereby creating a problem if the name is difficult to remember or not descriptive of the service (e.g., Rainbow House). This difficulty was offset only slightly by the fact that the provincial government department responsible for women's services provided a listing in each municipal phone directory for the nearest shelter under the heading of "wife assault help-line." The value of this approach is questionable since fewer than 1% of the women in our study who responded to this question thought to look under this term. Indeed, this example illustrates the confusion which faces women who may be attempting to deal with the maze of community services by using the telephone directory, which is one of the most commonly accessible information systems for the average person.

The results of the agency surveys revealed that, similar to the household respondents, human service providers tend to be unaware of public libraries and I & R centers as potential sources of help for making referrals. Fairly frequent mentions were made, however, of printed directories of community services (often described as "the red book," or the "little book" or "our list") although the agency respondents seemed to be unaware that these directories were often compiled by the community information center or library, nor did they mention that these organizations could be called for up-to-date or more detailed information about community services.

POTENTIAL ROLES FOR LIBRARIES

The findings of the two studies described here are somewhat discouraging in view of the current campaigns to promote public libraries as "the one place to look" (Ontario Public Library Strategic Planning Group, 1990). Although it is unreasonable to expect that a woman in a crisis situation would think of the public library as her first step in help-seeking, it is important for librarians to remember that assaulted women are not always in immediate danger. "Wife assault" is frequently pictured as an emergency situation, perhaps because both the research literature and the mass media tend to focus on women in shelters or on their interactions with the police. However, managing a life with a violent partner means that many women need information to cope with ongoing situations in which their needs may be as diverse as re-training for employment, assisting children to deal with the emotional aftermath of abuse, locating new housing, legal information pertinent to custody and access and/or property division, or, as Harris (1988) has shown, looking for answers to questions about their personal relationships.

In this context it is useful to remember that at least 50% of public library users are women. Given the current estimates of the incidence of wife assault, and its occurrence across all demographic categories, library staff must routinely encounter women who are in abusive situations. That is, whether they know it or not, public librarians are meeting battered women every day–women who are borrowing books, bringing their children to story hour, asking a reference question, or attending a book discussion.

Given this diversity of potential contact, LIS practitioners are uniquely placed in the community to play at least three fundamental but different roles in meeting the information needs that may arise from woman abuse. First, they may be able to provide information services directly to women who are currently experiencing violence or who may have been assaulted in the past. Second, librarians can be proactive in identifying and meeting the information needs of members of the human services network, i.e., people who work in social service agencies and professional practices. Third, libraries can play a role in serving the research needs of government, public and private funding agencies, and others who influence social policy and develop social services. Public libraries, especially those with well-developed I & R programs, can help all three client groups, but academic and special libraries also have a particular responsibility with respect to service providers and policy makers.

Information for Battered Women

Public libraries, owing to their community service mandate, must be prepared to provide (and to make it known that they provide) information to women who find themselves in abusive situations, as well as to their families and friends. The most critical information (see Harris, 1988, p. 69) is an accurate listing of community resources, including information about the location and nature of these services. Library staff themselves need to be more aware of the range of services available to battered women, including but not limited to crisis centers and emergency shelters. Many libraries already provide this type of information through their own I & R service (Durrance, 1984; Levinson, 1988), or through referrals to independent community information centers that can help women identify and gain access to the appropriate agencies. At the very least, public libraries should provide access to a directory or database of community services, even if the library does not itself participate in the collection of this information.

Sometimes library users *do* feel comfortable talking about their personal problems to library staff. Rather than viewing such accounts as social conversations to be curtailed as quickly as possible, staff should be alert to the expression of information needs, know the appropriate way to respond to such a situation and know how to make accurate referrals. Any service provider who comes into contact with a battered woman needs to know first how to assess the situation in terms of the woman's immediate safety, then how to find out what kind of help is wanted: this is done primarily by developing good listening and interview skills that show sensitivity and allow the woman to explain as much or as little of her situation as she wishes. In Dewdney and Harris (1992), emotional support was one of the three most frequently mentioned needs in situations involving abuse. Other studies, too, reveal that in order to be effective, information service delivery must address the affective or emotional as well as the cognitive or task-oriented aspects of information needs (see Harris and Dewdney, in press.)

Not surprisingly, most women who use the library to locate information about wife assault may not wish to identify themselves as being battered. It is, in fact, the perception of the public library as a neutral, anonymous and non-threatening institution that may be a key attraction for people who want to find information without disclosing their actual need to anyone else. As one librarian in our agency survey explained, a simple directional question such as "where is your legal section?" may mask a more complex inquiry about the rights of battered women. Library staff must recognize a user's need and right to maintain control over their own situations, even if that means not disclosing the basis of the inquiry.

Whether or not the purpose of a visit is disclosed, public libraries can nevertheless be helpful by making it easy for users to help themselves, through preparation, for example, of displays, booklists, pamphlet racks and informational programs for the general public through which users can become informed without explicitly asking for staff help. One critical element that determines ease of access for those who wish to help themselves is the quality of the library's catalog. For example, a woman interested in carrying out a subject search on the topic of wife assault is likely to encounter obstacles posed by the problematic current Library of Congress Subject Headings. The term "battered women" still does not appear as a heading in the 16th edition of the *Library of Congress Subject Headings* (1993), nor do the terms "battered women's services" or "violence against women," although these terms were recommended by Berman in 1984 and the National Women's Studies Association in 1988 (NWSA Resolution, 1990). Instead, the headings are "wife abuse," "abused wives" and "abused women"– terms that the casual user might not think of employing. Fortunately, the LC subject headings (LCSH) have been improved with the addition of "use" or "see" references from "battered wives" and "battered women" to the preferred terms previously mentioned. Furthermore, LCSH now include the subject heading "women's shelters" with a cross reference from the non-preferred term "battered women's shelters."

Although there is an attempt in the LC subject headings to guide users to the less common preferred terms (such as "wife abuse") through cross references from more colloquial terms (such as "bat-

tered women"), the capacity of casual users to find what they need is still questionable. First, many library catalogs do not display the syndetic structure (system of referrals from one term to another) of LCSH within them. In an online environment, this means that the user is given no guidance as to what the preferred terminology may be. Second, in order to search the subject catalog effectively, the user will need to understand the concept of a controlled vocabulary. If there are no cross-references in the catalog, users must be alerted to the fact that they will need to consult the LCSH before attempting a subject-oriented search. However, even if the cross-references are displayed in the catalog, understanding the controlled vocabulary itself is not necessarily self-evident. Users must decipher the associative relationships (broader or narrower terms) used in LCSH, and must use these terms to broaden or narrow the search appropriately. Therefore, it is quite likely that through the use of incorrect or inappropriate subject terminology, or through a general lack of understanding of the purpose and structure of a controlled vocabulary, the casual user will fail to find important sources of information.

In addition to access, librarians should be concerned about the collections available to users. For instance, library collections should contain both fiction and non-fiction materials that address women's questions about personal relationships. Librarians should not underestimate the value of fiction to people who are going through difficult times. For example, one woman in Harris's (1988) study mentioned that she read a lot of romance novels because she wanted to know that "life worked out for someone" (p. 67). Fiction reading can be especially effective in speaking directly to the reader's concerns because the reader's own preoccupations seem to work as a filter, according to Ross (1991) who has found through her own studies and through reviewing the literature of reading that books give people comfort, reassure them that they are normal, help them think clearly about their feelings, and give them strength and courage to make changes in their lives (p. 509).

Information for Service Providers

It was noted earlier that human service providers themselves do not always know how to respond appropriately to a request for help from a battered woman, and they may not be fully aware of other community resources. As Levinson (1988) points out:

> Among the first-contact agencies to whom people frequently turn for help with their problems are clergy, doctors, lawyers, and teachers, many of whom have need for information and referral services to carry out their professional and occupational service roles. Unaware of appropriate resources, community helpers tend to underutilize existing services or overutilize those services with which they are most familiar. . . . (p. 11)

Libraries can play a role in meeting the information needs of these "community helpers" by making community service directories available, by providing support materials for agency staff training, and by actively promoting current research literature on the problem of woman abuse. This potential continuing education function of libraries is particularly important for community professionals such as lawyers, physicians, clergy members and others who work in private practice and deal with a variety of social problems, as well as for those workers who are employed in agencies in which service to battered women is not the primary mandate.

It is not only public libraries that can provide support to direct service providers. Academic libraries, for example, not only support professional schools or community-oriented faculties or departments such as family medicine and counseling psychology, but they may also be a specialized resource for community workers who are not directly affiliated with a university. Such libraries have a responsibility not only to acquire but to make known (e.g., through current awareness services) relevant materials such as government reports and journals which either routinely or in theme issues deal with the subject of woman abuse.

Another type of library which appears to be underutilized in this context is the resource center which specializes in family violence or women's studies materials. In Canada, for example, the National Clearinghouse on Family Violence is an excellent resource for all kinds of published and unpublished material. It provides not only lists of current acquisitions and customized searches but also an extremely efficient document delivery service to individuals and agencies.[2] In the United States, the Clearinghouse on Family Violence Information, the Clearinghouse on Women's Issues, and the Center for Women's Studies and Services provide similar help.[3]

Librarians working in all types of libraries need to assist their own users to become more aware of the resources available to them. However, this does require improvements in the structuring of information systems to make them more responsive to inquiries about social problems. The difficulty of gaining access to journal literature on problems such as wife assault is evident even in the LIS field. For example, the *Library Literature* index on H.W. Wilson's CD-ROM provides access to our research (Harris, 1988; Harris and Dewdney, 1991; Dewdney and Harris, 1992) only through the subject heading "information services/special subjects/women" without any cross reference from related headings except "women." This suggests that our own literature on information needs that are associated with human problems is classified so broadly as to make access virtually impossible without knowing the names of authors or titles of specific articles. In this sense, then, subject retrieval of appropriate documents seems to depend, as was the case with the telephone book, on lucky guesses.

Information for Policy Makers and Funders

Much of the information needed by service providers is also useful to policy makers and funding authorities. Obvious examples include statistics on the incidence of battering and the implications for economic or social policy, new research into causes and preventative aspects of violence against women, reports which identify gaps in community services, as well as descriptions and evaluations of model programs. The potential role for libraries in managing this information is obvious, particularly given the significant increase in the quantity of literature on woman abuse that is being generated by governments, academic researchers and private consultants, as well as individual service agencies. Librarians in a variety of settings could play a useful role by acting as quality filters for this literature and making it promptly and easily accessible since some of the most useful material, such as consultants' reports, is not indexed.

ROLES FOR LIBRARY AND INFORMATION SCIENCE: CONSULTING AND RESEARCH

Beyond traditional library functions, LIS practitioners may be of use in linking assaulted women to appropriate help resources by taking on other roles.

The Information Management Role

The first and most obvious expertise that librarians have to offer is an extensive knowledge of and experience in organizing any kind of information so that it can be easily retrieved and used. This means a capacity to make more accessible to service providers and policy makers the existing research on battered women, which is increasingly found in a large number of different subject areas. However, as illustrated with respect to the LC subject headings, this expertise is not always used in such a way as to make it easy for library users to gain subject access themselves. This problem occurs in catalogs and indexes, in both print and electronic form, which may be used by non-specialist librarians or the end user. Clearly, LIS specialists interested in social issues could make a considerable contribution by using their expertise to make information on such topics more accessible.

Information management skills can also be used to assist service providers to organize more effectively their own agency information. This could involve providing records management expertise to organizations such as women's shelters that often accumulate significant information about their client and community profiles. Easy retrieval of such information is essential to the planning and accountability functions of these agencies.

Independent I & R centers also have a need for expertise in building databases for community information, with usable thesauri that can be standardized or customized to list types of services as well as individual agencies. Although it may seem obvious to librarians that authority control is an essential component of any effective information retrieval system, this may be a novel concept to I & R center managers.

LIS practitioners could also lend their expertise to the construction of local telephone directories. The difficulties faced by service providers and their clients in finding relevant information in these directories arises from basic problems of classification and indexing. Clearly, what is needed is to devise a system that allows multiple access points to agency names when a person is searching for a particular type of help but is unaware of agencies that provide that type of assistance. In the absence of such a system, it is important for individual agencies to understand how and where to list their services in the telephone book. For instance, some community information services and social service agencies are now listing their phone numbers under help-related subject terms rather than agency names (e.g., battered women's shelter, or counseling instead of Rainbow House) or they have purchased "see" references in both the white and yellow pages of the telephone directory.

The Research Role

More than any other discipline, LIS is suited to developing a body of theoretical knowledge about information needs and information-seeking behavior in a variety of settings. Although much of the LIS work in this area to date has been focused on the work-related information needs of scholars and professionals (see, for example, review articles on information needs and uses in the *Annual Review of Information Science and Technology*), an increasing amount of attention is currently being paid to the information needs of ordinary people, which is the knowledge needed to design responsive human services systems (Dervin and Nilan, 1986). Through our own research and studies of help-seeking behavior in psychology, medical sociology and communications, for example, some basic principles of human information seeking behavior have been identified (Harris and Dewdney, in press, 1994). These include the recognition that information needs are situationally based, that both the affective as well as the cognitive dimensions of information needs require attention, the importance of physical, intellectual and cultural accessibility, the perceived personal risks in information-seeking, and the inclination of citizens to use informal rather than formal information systems.

LIS professionals who are interested in enhancing information systems for social services can undertake research can be done at an applied level (i.e., to define or solve immediate problems in real situations) or at a "pure" level. However, in order to develop a meaningful research agenda, it is essential to build on a workable concept of information from the user's point of view. This means broadening our understanding of information by looking not simply at situations in which a person in need intersects with our existing systems, but studying the contexts in which the information needs initially arise.

CONCLUSION

It is clear that librarians have the potential to make a variety of important contributions to overcoming the information-related issues associated with problems such as woman abuse. However, this requires a willingness to develop an understanding of social issues, a new orientation to research (as consumers and investigators), and a commitment to reaching out to others in the community, both clients and other human service providers, to take a proactive stance with respect to the facilitation of information or help-seeking.

NOTES

1. Community information center is a term used in Canada for what are generally known as information and referral (I & R) centers in the United States, and Citizens' Advisory Bureaux in the United Kingdom.

2. National Clearinghouse on Family Violence, Room 1114, Finance Building, Tunney's Pasture, Ottawa, Canada KLA 183.

3. The current edition of the *Encyclopedia of Associations* or the *Directory of Special Libraries and Information Centers* will provide addresses and descriptions for those centers.

REFERENCES

Beal, Christina (1979). Studying the public's information needs. *Journal of Librarianship*, 11(2), 130-151.

Berman, Sanford (1984). Out of the kitchen–But not into the catalog. *Technical Services Quarterly*, 2 (167-171).

Chen, Ching-chih and Hernon, Peter (1982). *Information seeking: Assessing and anticipating user needs.* New York: Neal-Schuman.

Dervin, Brenda (1983). Information as user construct: The relevance of perceived information needs to synthesis and interpretation. In S.A. Ward and L.J. Reed (eds.), *Knowledge structure and use: Implications for synthesis and interpretation*. Philadelphia, PA: Temple University Press, 155-183.

Dervin, Brenda and Nilan, Michael (1986). Information needs and uses. In Martha E. Williams (ed.), *Annual Review of Information Science and Technology, Vol. 21*. White Plains, NY: Knowledge Industry Publications, 3-33.

Dewdney, Patricia and Harris, Roma M. (1992). Community information needs: The case of wife assault. *Library & Information Science Research, 14*(5-29).

Durrance, Joan C. (1984). Community information services: An innovation at the beginning of its second decade. In *Advances in Librarianship, Vol. 13*. New York: Academic Press, 99-128.

Greaves, Lorraine, Heapy, Nelson, and Wylie, Alison (1988). Advocacy services: Reassessing the profile and needs of battered women. *Canadian Journal of Community Mental Health, 7*(2), 39-51.

Harris, Roma M. (1988). The information needs of battered women. *RQ, 28*, 62-70.

Harris, Roma M., and Dewdney, Patricia (1991). Exchanging information about wife assault: A mismatch of citizen needs and social service system response. *Canadian Library Journal, 48*, 407-411.

Harris, Roma M., and Dewdney, Patricia (in press, 1994). *Barriers to Information: How Formal Help Systems Fail Battered Women*. Westport, CT: Greenwood Press.

Homer, Marjorie, Leonard, Anne, and Taylor, Pat (1985). Personal relationships: help and hindrance. In Norman Johnson (ed.), *Sociological Review Monograph 31, Marital Violence*. London: Routledge and Kegan Paul, 93-108.

Johnson, Norman (1985). Police, social work and medical responses to battered women. In Norman Johnson (ed.), *Sociological Review Monograph 31, Marital Violence*. London: Routledge and Kegan Paul, 109-123.

Lazarus, Richard S. and Folkman, Susan (1984). Coping and adaptation. In W. Doyle Gentry (ed.), *Handbook of behavioral medicine*. New York: Guilford Press, 282-325.

Levinson, R. W. (1988). *Information and Referral Networks: Doorways to Human Services*. Springer Series on Social Work, Vol. 10. New York: Springer Publishing Company.

Library of Congress Cataloging Distribution Service (1993). *Library of Congress Subject Headings*. 16th ed. Vols. 1-4. Washington, DC.

MacLeod, Linda (1989). *The City for Women: No Safe Place*. A paper funded by the Corporate Policy Branch, Secretary of State Canada, for the European and North American Conference on Urban Safety and Crime Prevention, Montreal, Quebec.

National Women's Studies Association (1990). NWSA resolution: sexism in LC subject headings [reprinted from *WLW Journal*, Fall '88]. In Sanford Berman and James P. Danky (eds.), *Alternative Library Literature, 1988/1989*. Jefferson, NC: McFarland & Company, Inc., 22.

Ontario Public Library Strategic Planning Group (1990). *One Place to Look.* Toronto: Ontario Ministry of Culture and Communications.

Ross, Catherine Sheldrick (1991). Readers' advisory service: New directions. *RQ*, 30, 503-518.

Trute, Barry, Sarsfield, Peter, and MacKenzie, Dale A. (1988). Medical response to wife abuse: A survey of physicians' attitudes and practices. *Canadian Journal of Community Mental Health, 7*(2), 61-71.

Trute, Barry, Sarsfield, Peter, and MacKenzie, Dale A. (1988). Medical response to wife abuse: A survey of physicians' attitudes and practices, *Canadian Journal of Community Mental Health, 7*(2), 61-71.

Walker, Lenore (1984). *The Battered Woman Syndrome.* New York: Springer Publishing Company.

Information Needs of Special Populations: Serving People with Mental Illnesses Using Computer Aided Instruction in a Multimedia Library for Outpatients

Adele L. Barsh
Meliza Jackson

SUMMARY. The interactive presentation of information has special utility for individuals with cognitive disorders who may experience difficulty processing information from books. This article reports on a use of computer-aided instruction (CAI) and multimedia technology to meet the information needs of a special population–people who have severe and persistent mental illnesses.

LSCA Title I monies funded this alternative approach to traditional institutional library services to explore the promise held by CAI for helping thought-disordered patrons internalize information, in this case on consumer health and vocational topics. Described here are this population's special needs, the rationale for services to be tailored accordingly, uses of computers in psychiatric rehabilitation, collection development and usage, and reaction to the project. *[Article copies available from The Haworth Document Delivery Service: 1-800-342-9678.]*

Adele L. Barsh is Reference Librarian at Robert Morris College in Pittsburgh, PA. She has also served as Western Psychiatric Institute and Clinic (WPIC) Outpatients' Librarian since 1933. Meliza Jackson directed Patients' Libraries services for 15 years at WPIC, where the mailing address is 3501 Forbes Avenue, Pittsburgh, PA 15213.

[Haworth co-indexing entry note]: "Information Needs of Special Populations: Serving People with Mental Illnesses Using Computer Aided Instruction in a Multimedia Library for Outpatients." Barsh, Adele L. and Meliza Jackson. Co-published simultaneously in *The Reference Librarian* (The Haworth Press, Inc.) No. 53, 1996, pp. 47-61; and: *Reference Services for the Unserved* (ed: Fay Zipkowitz) The Haworth Press, Inc., 1996, pp. 47-61. Single or multiple copies of this article are available from The Haworth Document Delivery Service: [1-800-342-9678, 9:00 a.m. - 5:00 p.m. (EST)].

The Outpatients' Library of Western Psychiatric Institute and Clinic (WPIC) is a non-traditional library that serves a special needs population, namely people with major mental illnesses. Resources of the Outpatients' Library are primarily electronic, including computer programs, interactive laserdiscs, CD-ROM products, and videocassettes. The Library's resources focus on vocational rehabilitation and consumer health issues.

The Library project developed when WPIC Library staff recognized the potential of interactive media for outpatients and applied for Library Services and Construction Act (LSCA) funds for the project. This article will explain the project and highlight aspects of it of general interest to librarians. The Outpatient Library project should prove informative to library professionals because, as one commentator observes:

> With the continuing trend of deinstitutionalizing persons with physical, mental, and emotional disabilities, and the development of community-based housing and social services to these populations, libraries are now acquiring potential users with special needs which many libraries and their collective staffs are ill-prepared to serve. (Zipkowitz, 1991, p. 53)

PROJECT OVERVIEW

WPIC houses the Department of Psychiatry of the University of Pittsburgh School of Medicine. The clinical, teaching, and research arms of WPIC provide psychiatric specialty services under the aegis of the University of Pittsburgh Medical Center. A regional referral center for the 23 counties of western Pennsylvania and the adjacent areas of Ohio and West Virginia, WPIC serves a diverse population.

The Schizophrenia Treatment and Research Center (STRC) is the outpatient division of one of WPIC's major treatment modules, the Schizophrenia Module. STRC, located a few blocks away from the main hospital, houses the Outpatients' Library. Although the majority of the Library's patrons have schizophrenia, the Library serves clients of other WPIC treatment modules, including mental retardation, depression and other mood disorders, substance abuse, and dual diagnoses.

The Outpatients' Library was established in July 1991 with monies from a grant from the State Library of Pennsylvania funded by LSCA, Title I. The grant was to launch a demonstration program for library services to people with serious and persistent mental illnesses. Grant funding paid for equipment, software, and part-time staff. WPIC contributed part-time staff, a small facility, utilities, and other in-kind support. Start up equipment included an early-generation multimedia IBM-PC (PS-2 Multimedia M57SLC with touchscreen capability), an IBM clone (Dell 325D, a "286" PC), a Hewlett-Packard LaserJetIII printer, a Pioneer Level III laserdisc player (LDV-4400), a Panasonic 13″ television monitor, a Macintosh LC series PC, and an Apple II computer. Grant activities included developing the collection's initial bibliography and hosting six demonstration days and a statewide institution librarians' meeting.

The following year, Library staff applied for and received a different but complementary LSCA grant to train librarians in the use of computer-aided instruction (CAI) and interactive laserdisc technology. The goal was to improve access to prevocational and wellness information–not only for clients served by the project, but also on a statewide level, through public and institution librarians. During this grant year, collection development focused on consumer health information. A printer (HP LaserJet 4L) and a Level II laserdisc player (Pioneer LDV6000) were purchased, and a PC (ATT 6386SX/EL) was received as a donation. A workshop to train 80 librarians was held in conjunction with The Carnegie Library of Pittsburgh. The original bibliography was updated, and the revised two-catalog set was distributed to over 400 public and institution libraries in Pennsylvania in 1994. Information about the catalogs is available from Meliza Jackson, Director of WPIC Patients' Libraries.

SPECIAL NEEDS RELATED TO SCHIZOPHRENIA

According to the National Alliance for the Mentally Ill, mental illness is a term used to describe disorders that cause severe disturbances in thinking, feeling, and relating. Major types of mental illness are often grouped in three categories: schizophrenia, mood disorders, and other severe conditions, such as anxiety disorders or substance abuse disorders. Serious mental illnesses interfere with a person's ability to function in daily life, and usually require ongoing treatment.

Mental illness occurs across all age, gender, race, ethnic, and class groups. Approximately 30 to 45 million Americans, about 1 in 5, have a form of mental illness that requires professional treatment. About 12 million children have various mental illnesses. Eight to 14 million Americans experience depression each year, and more than 2 million Americans will be diagnosed with schizophrenia during their lifetimes (National Institute of Mental Health [NIMH], 1991; Torrey, Wolfe, & Flynn, 1988).

Schizophrenia occurs in only about 1% of the population both in the United States and worldwide, but on any given day, 30%-50% of the U.S. psychiatric facility spaces are devoted to people with schizophrenia (Torrey et al., 1988). In the U.S., schizophrenia " . . . is five times more common than multiple sclerosis, six times more so than insulin-dependent diabetes, and 60 times more so than muscular dystrophy" (Torrey et al., 1988, p. 2).

Schizophrenia is not a single disease, but a cluster of disorders with shared symptoms that affect a person's intellectual, emotional, and social functioning. Specifically, the mental processes involved in sensation, perception, language, emotion, and interpersonal relations are altered (NIMH, 1991). Hallmarks include disordered thinking, delusions, false sensory experiences, and emotional inappropriateness. A person with schizophrenia may have trouble with inferential and abstract thinking, or experience a loss of the sense of boundaries between self and others. Drive, volition, and concentration are often impaired. Violence is not typical of schizophrenia. Despite media depictions to the contrary,

> In the great majority of cases, the image of the former mental patient as a homicidal maniac in need of restraint is far from the truth. . . . Of a sample of some 20,000 former mental patients monitored for 18 months after their release from hospitals, only 33 were arrested for crimes involving violence. (NIMH, 1988, p. 11)

No one symptom is the litmus test, but psychotic symptoms are an important consideration in diagnosis. In the acute phase, such symptoms can include delusions or hallucinations, or disorganized speech. Effects and duration of acute symptoms vary. Some people remain severely and persistently ill, while others go through periods of worsening symptoms followed by remissions. A person with severe and persistent symptoms usually does not fully recover, and long-term treatment, medication, and repeated hospitalizations are required to control symptoms (NIMH, 1986).

Onset is typically experienced in men during their teens and twenties, and in women during their twenties and thirties. Although the causes of schizophrenia are believed to be biological, the specifics are not yet fully understood. To complicate matters further, the cause may vary dependent on type of symptom group. Some recognized biological mechanisms are changes in the brain's anatomy, chemistry, and metabolism. Medications block some symptoms, but effectiveness varies among individuals, and many have serious side effects. They do not cure the disease.

SERVICE RATIONALE OF THE OUTPATIENTS' LIBRARY

The great majority of Library clients have schizophrenia. Library services were designed to contribute to their psychiatric rehabilitation, which can be defined as a process that " . . . assists persons with long-term psychiatric disabilities to increase their functioning so that they are successful and satisfied in the environments of their choice with the least amount of ongoing professional intervention" (Anthony & Cohen & Farkas, 1990, p. 2). In the recent past, rehabilitation more often was seen as a means to an end. Psychiatric rehabilitation professionals now recognize that the interaction of a person's disabilities and social environment is an ongoing process subject to cyclical elements (Watts, 1991, p. xiv). Recent national policy statements about services for and research on mental illness reflect this newer paradigm of rehabilitation and emphasize the scientific scrutiny of services. A 1991 document by NIMH policy makers recommends:

> With any illness, but especially with [mental] disorders that endure and disable people, providing the right medication is essential, but not enough. A full range of services attending to rehabilitation, independent living, and enhanced quality of

life is needed. Finding ways to improve the standard of care and ways to provide it through better organization and financing of services are compelling public health needs. (NIMH, 1991, p. vii)

STRC is a strong example of such comprehensive programming: services include one-on-one therapeutic relationships, medical follow-up, skills training, arts therapies, and structured social activities. STRC is the location for the offices of doctors, clinicians, group therapists, and intensive case managers; rooms for activities; the Outpatients' Library; and a client-run snack shop. Skills training classes include word processing and computing. A partial list of groups includes art, music, movement, money management, nutrition and health, recreational activities, current events, literacy, mathematics, parenting, spirituality, dual diagnoses issues, women's issues, and relapse prevention. The Library has a collection of software that can tie in with most groups.

COMPUTERS IN MENTAL HEALTH REHABILITATION

Rehabilitative projects in mental health that use computer technology began in the late 1970s and early 1980s. Therapists used computers in rehabilitation support activities such as billing, note-taking and tracking clients (Anthony et al., 1990; Lawrence, 1986). Projects in which clients had direct contact with the computer also developed. One well-known example that emulated a one-on-one session with a therapist was ELIZA, a program written by MIT computer scientist Joseph Weizenbaum (Bluhm, 1988; Lawrence, 1986).

Computers were well-accepted and successfully used in client vocational projects. Some focused on teaching computer skills in order to make clients more competitive in the job market (Jofre, 1988). Others used computers to assess career goals, define and teach job skills, assist in job hunting, and perform other employment support activities (Midgley, 1990). The Library follows the latter model, offering resume-making, job descriptions, stress management, interviewing practice, and career and educational exploration. Users learn computer skills only secondarily.

Use of computers has expanded into patient education (Jelovsek &

Adebonojo, 1993; Kahn, 1993; Petzel, Ellis, Budd, & Johnson, 1992). Several studies have shown that patient education, computerized or not, reduces medication non-compliance (Kahn, 1993, p. 94). A meta-analysis of research showed high non-compliance among people with schizophrenia: 11-80% within the first year, 74% within the first two years of treatment (Corrigan & Liberman & Engle, 1990, p. 1203). Medication is often able to relieve the most disruptive symptoms, but several barriers to compliance exist (Corrigan et al., 1990; Weiden & Havens, 1994). Comprehensive treatment programs where clients take active roles in their treatment have been most effective (Corrigan et al., 1990).

Two WPIC Schizophrenia Module psychiatrists–T. Bradley Tanner, MD, and Stuart Gitlow, MD–co-wrote and produced a hypercard program for the Macintosh called *Medication Education: Educating the Psychiatric Patient*, or *Med Ed*. Available in the Outpatients' Library for STRC internal use, the program explains the purpose of taking haloperidol and fluphenazine, two often-prescribed neuroleptics. Verbally and visually, *Med Ed* describes both how to take medication and its side effects. The user selects which drug to learn about, then what type of information is needed. Color graphics, sound, and video clips convey the information.

A program such as *Med Ed* is typical of multimedia CAI in that it exploits the computer's ability to educate as it presents information via several types of communication channels. A CAI program allows input, and responds with information based on that input (Bolwell, 1988). A user can get "immediate, explanatory feedback, repetition of basic concepts after an incorrect response, provision of a comfortable learning environment, and linking of teaching material with learning objectives" (Jelovsek & Adebonojo, 1993, p. 165).

Another good example of CAI is the interactive laserdisc, *Getting Out and Staying Out: the Story of Cathy* (Olevitch, in press; Olevitch & Hagan, 1990, 1991). This program features Cathy leaving a psychiatric hospital. The user watches video clips and is asked to make decisions for Cathy during her first days out, inputting them to the computer. The user faces decisions through Cathy's eyes regarding taking medication regularly, interacting with others, and managing daily routines. The user's choices at branches in the program's storyline determine whether Cathy does well outside or goes back to the hospital. The user can repeat the program with different choices to see how changes affect the outcome. In this way, the CAI simulation "[provides] sheltered opportunities to make decisions and experience the consequences with the hope that there will be carry over to real life" (Harris-Bowlsbey, 1983, p. 12).

Some studies showed that users learned more from CAI than from typical instruction modes, especially if CAI involves laserdisc or videotape interactivity (Petty & Rosen, 1987; Zimmerman, 1988). Bolwell (1988) reminded readers that the learning objective should be foremost in choosing a mode of instructional delivery, computer-aided or not. Carlson (1991) found that CAI with interactive laserdisc programs worked best when well-matched with program content, and was not necessarily the best choice in all cases. Other researchers took a more cautionary stance after reviewing 30 years' worth of evaluative studies, saying that CAI has no significant advantages over other learning methods (Yildiz & Atkins, 1993).

The experience of the Outpatients' Library staff is that multimedia CAI is a very useful alternative method of learning for many clients. This was confirmed recently by Fine (1994), who reports on a similar comprehensive rehabilitation project for people with schizophrenia run by New York Hospital-Cornell University Medical Center. CAI was an integral part of a program used to teach clients cognitive and social skills, such as information processing, self-monitoring, and interpersonal skills. The goal of using CAI was to build a client's efficiency and flexibility in dealing with day to day tasks in both clinical and community settings. Since CAI programs are adaptable in content and format, they provide a structured and controllable means of teaching tasks which "makes possible learning of new or different cognitive skills and mental strategies" (Fine, 1994, p. 99). Clients are able to determine what tasks to work on and for how long; and the CAI format allows them to circumvent some of the environmental stimuli which can exacerbate the symptoms of schizophrenia.

COLLECTION DEVELOPMENT

Although research findings on the effectiveness of interactive multimedia are mixed, and little research has been done regarding its use with people with mental illnesses, Library staff anticipated that the special features of multimedia would work well with STRC's clients. As one mental health professional put it, cognitive habilitation of people with schizophrenia, in general, is:

> an interaction between patient and environment, designed and mediated by clinicians. While this environment need not be tied to a technology, computers can provide valuable assessment data and remediative experiences. . . . They can simulate attention tasks that require vigilance and measure the result with great accuracy . . . [and] computer environments can be highly predictable–thus facilitating organized thinking in relatively disorganized patients. This predictability can be highly rewarding and motivating. (Flesher, 1990, p. 224)

The first major collection development issue was that the Library needed to have computers and equipment that ran multimedia formats. The computers needed to run interactive laserdisc and CD-ROM programs, which feature presentation of content accompanied by combinations of video, sound, text, and clear and interesting graphics. Such programming was highly organized and offered individualized presentations, which had obvious potential for use with people who have short attention spans, low reading skills, motivation problems, or disorganized thinking. Programs that used a touch-screen and a combined audio/video presentation also bypassed many physical limitations. Many patrons do not have previous computer experience, and most interactive laserdiscs and CD-ROMs take that into account. The Library can run programs on two types, or levels, of laserdiscs. As typical, the Library's multimedia PC (MPC) also runs CD-ROMs. Staff found that they wanted the flexibility to run CAI programs that existed for Apple, Macintosh, and "regular" PCs, and acquired that equipment, as well.

Once staff decided on equipment, they faced another major issue in collection development: finding resources suited to the Library's clientele. The selection process was difficult because clients vary in educational background, reading level, experience, job skills, symptoms, race, culture, gender, age, and interests. The collection had to reflect this variety. Staff had to avoid assumptions that oversimplified and patronized clients' abilities and interests.

Library staff targeted vocational software distributors and producers through locating sources such as *Computer Use in Psychology: a Directory of Software*, *Psychware Sourcebook*, *CD-ROM Information Products*, and *Video Source Book*. Hundreds of software titles were considered. Over 100 were acquired after being previewed and evaluated against a software evaluation checklist which analyzed technical merits, content, and presentation. Collection development for wellness software began in 1992; over 100 titles were purchased. The vocational resource catalogs also yielded leads for wellness resources. Locating tools included *Interactive Health Care Directory*, *Software for Health Sciences Education: a Resource Catalog*, and reviews like Hsu's "Dr. Computer."

Available resources tended to fall into groups by intended audience. Only two programs in the whole collection were specifically designed for people with a mental illness: *Med Ed* and *Cathy*. Vocational resources for adults often had a "fast lane" approach: those programs' producers assumed the adult audience had high motivation and strong job skills. Vocational programs that started with basic skills or accommodated lower reading levels usually had a bias toward high school users, which was reflected in program content and language. Some programs had technical problems, or made poor graphic presentations. Some less desirable programs were collected if a unique feature outweighed the negative qualities. For example, an interactive laserdisc was purchased even though it featured recent high school graduates, because it provided useful exercises in critical thinking on the job. Staff running the program tried to compensate for shortcomings.

The wellness collection also reflected the market bias of producers. Programs covering drug use and abuse, pregnancy, and self-esteem were aimed at high school students. Programs that treated medical topics in depth, intended for health professionals, could be too complex. Although there were several new CD-ROMs for the home consumer which were good overall in graphics and multimedia effects, they were for the most part too general. Another drawback of commercial wellness offerings was their reflection of fads, such as diet and nutrition programs. They less often addressed what might be deemed less marketable issues, such as mental health.

LIBRARY USAGE

Perhaps the greatest difficulty faced in serving clients is the nature of their illnesses. Some clients are unable to concentrate or follow a set routine, have unrealistic expectations, or experience rehospitalization, all of which disrupt rehabilitation services. Many have difficulty remembering appointments or keeping themselves motivated to come to them. Clients can choose to attend leisure activity programs taking place during Library hours, which can be more entertaining diversions and less work.

Clinicians refer their clients to the Library, and help to schedule the appointments, but some clients drop in. Program selection can be highly individual, based on clients' interests and clinicians' recommendations. Software can either be coordinated with or used independent of the clients' other activities. Often staff get to know clients and explore several program types, based on mutual negotiation.

In 1992, staff surveyed STRC doctors and clinicians about the effectiveness of clients' use of Library resources. The survey asked respondents to rate their clients' interest and improvement in the areas of literacy, cognitive skills, vocational direction, job application, resume development, community coping skills, stress management, social skills, grooming, and substance abuse. The seventeen respondents were unanimous in their support for the program. Clients who used the Library regularly for two or three visits per week improved skills markedly, they said.

Staff began a "marketing campaign" aimed at increasing clinician support and gaining new patrons, including mood disorder clinic clients. Surveyed clinicians said that they relied on the resource catalogs and the recommendations of the Library staff to individualize plans for their clients. The campaign forged even closer working relationships with more doctors and clinicians: Four WPIC doctors outside STRC requested tours of the Library; clinician referrals to the library increased one-third; and there was an increase in walk-in clients and word-of-mouth referrals. After being publicized, the wellness resources proved themselves of interest to an even larger number of WPIC staff than were the vocational resources.

Close working relationships with the vocational counselors have benefitted both clients and staff. During 1993-94, 99 STRC clients received career counseling and other vocational services. Participants in groups such as Job Club and Work Support Group learn about the Library resources from peers and clinicians. The Library offers specialty services such as resume writing, design, and updates, help with cover letters, practice for interviewing, and contact information for potential employers. The successful outreach to vocational groups is being expanded to other sets of clients, such as those in the groups that focus on recovery from drug and alcohol abuse, stress management, nutrition, and women's issues. To facilitate clinician input, updated copies of the resource catalogs are circulated. Library staff announces new acquisitions at STRC staff meetings, and by automated phone system messages. Clinicians who are responsible for orienting new clients to STRC now regularly stop at the Library during their tours, and introduce clients and staff to each other.

REACTION TO THE PROJECT

Since they emphasize outpatient support, the Library's services are in tune with health care reform. How do rehabilitation services offered by the Outpatients Library mesh with other services and rehabilitation programs? Research shows that treatment delivery systems which incorporate independent living skills in a comprehensive way have been found to be useful (Corrigan et al., 1990), and those approaches that " . . . offer a number of services have generally been found to work better than those that offer only one or two" (NIMH, 1991). The National Plan of Research (NIMH, 1991) guidelines suggest quantifying the effects of various types of rehabilitative services. Library staff believes what it does has a beneficial effect on clients. How to identify and quantify that effect is important to consider.

Outreach to institutional and public libraries has been important to promote understanding of this clientele and the potential uses of multimedia technology. Interaction with the library community has directly resulted in three new programs at Pennsylvania state hospitals in 1994, and one in 1995, being patterned on the WPIC model. The resource catalogs have reached service providers in fields outside mental health, such as other types of rehabilitative services and public libraries.

Being a prototypical program has meant that staff often encounter situations which they must solve with creativity. The overall experience of the staff has been a maddening mix of excitement over the potential of the media vs. frustration over the difficulties of getting the technical components with a unusual configuration to function with one another.

The collection that resulted from this project is unique, but acquiring it and producing the bibliographies was staff-intensive. Selection, although based on sound library and rehabilitation principles, was largely experimental. Research devoted to use of such resources by people with mental illness is nearly non-existent. Although research does point out that CAI which teaches coping skills and problem solving is highly useful to persons with chronic illness and their families, developing such lessons in software form is difficult and time consuming (Petzel et al., 1992). Unanswered questions remain: What learning needs do outpatients have? In the absence of programs geared specifically for outpatients, should the Library get involved in designing programs? Given the requirements in time and resources, would it be better to continue working with and improving use of the programs at hand?

What has it been like to be a model project in providing Library services to people with major mental illnesses? It has been an effort of synthesizing methods from the fields of both library science and psychiatric rehabilitation. Outreach has been an important element in this process on several levels. Visibility within WPIC has been important to attract clients and establish the Library's role in treatment. Institutional support for the Library has increased so that at the end of 1994 it moved into new and larger facilities. The new location is more easily accessible to treatment modules other than STRC's, which is leading in turn to a larger role for the Outpatient Library at WPIC.

REFERENCES

Anthony, W., Cohen, M., & Farkas, M. (1990). *Psychiatric rehabilitation*. Boston: Center for Psychiatric Rehabilitation.

Armstrong, C.J. & Large, J.A. (Eds.). (1990). *CD-ROM information products: an evaluation guide and directory*. Brookfield, VT: Gower Publishing Company.

Bluhm, H.P. (1988). *Computers in guidance, counseling, and psychotherapy*. Springfield, IL: Thomas.

Bolwell, C. (1988). Evaluating computer-assisted instruction. *Nursing and Health Care*, *9*(9), 511-15.

Brown, C. et al. *Vocational evaluation systems and software: a consumer's guide.* (1994). Menomonie, WI: University of Wisconsin-Stout.

Carlson, H. (1991). Learning style and program design in interactive multimedia. *Educational Technology Research and Development*, *39*(3), 41-8.

Corrigan, P.W., Liberman, R.P., & Engle, J.D. (1990). From noncompliance to collaboration in the treatment of schizophrenia. *Hospital and Community Psychiatry*, *41*(11), 1203-11.

Fine, S. B. (1994). Reframing rehabilitation: putting skill acquisition and the mental health system into proper perspective. In W. E. Spaulding (Ed.). *Cognitive technology in psychiatric rehabilitation* (pp. 87-113). Lincoln, NE: University of Nebraska Press.

Flesher, S. (1990). Cognitive habilitation in schizophrenia: a theoretical review and model of treatment. *Neuropsychology Review*, *1*(3), 223-246.

Harris-Bowlsbey, J. (1983). The computer and the decider. *The Counseling Psychologist*, *11*(4), 9-14.

Hsu, J. (1993). Dr. Computer. *American Health*, *85*(September), 72-6.

Interactive health care directory. (1992). Alexandria, VA: Stewart Publishing, Inc.

Jelovsek, F. R., & Adebonojo, L. (1993). Learning principles as applied to computer-assisted instruction. *MD Computing*, *10*(3), 165-72.

Jofre, S. (1988). Computers for psychiatric patients. *New Statesman & Society*, *1*(June 24), 31.

Kahn, G. (1993). Computer-based patient education: a progress report. *MD Computing*, *10*(2), 93-9.

Krug, S.E. (Ed.). (1988). *Psychware Sourcebook*. Kansas City, MO: Test Corporation of America.

Lawrence, G.H. (1986). Using computers for the treatment of psychological problems. *Computers in Human Behavior*, *2*, 43-62.

Learning Resource Center, University of Michigan Medical Center. (1993). *Software for health sciences education: a resource catalog* (4th ed.). Ann Arbor, MI: University of Michigan Press.

Midgley, G. (1990). Developments in IT training for people with disabilities. *Behavior and Information Technology*, *9*(5), 397-407.

National Institute of Mental Health. (1986). *Schizophrenia: questions and answers.* Bethesda, MD: National Institute of Mental Health. DHHS Publication No. (ADM) 86-1457.

National Institute of Mental Health. (1988). *The 14 worst myths about recovered mental patients.* Bethesda, MD: National Institute of Mental Health. DHHS Publication No. (ADM) 88-1391.

National Institute of Mental Health, National Advisory Mental Health Council. (1991). *Caring for people with severe mental disorders: a national plan of research to improve services.* Bethesda, MD: National Institute of Mental Health. DHHS Publication No. (ADM) 91-1762.

Olevitch, B. (in press). *Cognitive approaches to the seriously mentally ill: dialogue across the barrier.* Westport, CT: Praeger Publishers.

Olevitch, B. & Hagan, B.J. (1990). "How to get out and stay out": an educational videodisc for the chronically mentally ill. *Computers in Human Services,* 5(3/4), 57-69.

Olevitch, B. & Hagan, B.J. (1991). An interactive videodisc as a tool in the rehabilitation of the chronically mentally ill: a preliminary investigation. *Computers in Human Behavior,* 7(1/2), 57-73.

Petty, L.C. & Rosen, E.F. (1987). Computer-based interactive video systems. *Behavior research methods, instruments and Computers,* 19, 160-66.

Petzel, S.V., Ellis, L.B.M., Budd, J.R., & Johnson, Y. (1992). Microcomputers for behavioral health education: developing and evaluating patient education for the chronically ill. *Computer Applications in Mental Health,* 8(3/4), 167-83.

Stoloff, M.L. & Couch, J.V. (1988). *Computer use in psychology: a directory of software* (2nd ed.). Washington, DC: American Psychological Association.

Torrey, E.F., Wolfe, S.M., & Flynn, L.M. (1988). *Care of the seriously mentally ill: a rating of state programs* (2nd ed). Alexandria, VA: Public Citizen Health Research Group and National Association for the Mentally Ill.

Video source book (12th ed). (1990). Syosset, NY: National Video Clearinghouse.

Wallis, C. & Willwerth, J. (1992). Schizophrenia. *Time,* (July 5), 53-7.

Watts, F. N. (1991) Employment. In Watts, F.N. & Bennet, D.H. (Eds.), *Theory and practice of psychiatric rehabilitation* (2nd ed). (pp. 215-240). NY: Wiley & Sons.

Weiden, P. & Havens, L. (1994) Psychotherapeutic management techniques in the treatment of outpatients with schizophrenia. *Hospital & Community Psychiatry,* 45(6), 549-555.

Yildiz, R., & Atkins, M. (1993). Evaluating multimedia applications. *Computers and Education,* 21(July-September), 133-9.

Zimmerman, S.O. (1988). Problem-solving tasks on the microcomputer: a look at the performance of students with learning disabilities. *Journal of Learning Disabilities,* 21(December), 637-41.

Zipkowitz, F. (1991). "No one wants to see them": Meeting the reference needs of the deinstitutionalized. *The Reference Librarian,* 31, 53-67.

Library Services
to Traditionally Underserved Groups:
An Annotated Bibliography

Rashelle S. Karp
Patricia L. Horne

INTRODUCTION

Library literature in the last few years has begun to reflect librarians' experience with serving hitherto unserved populations in a variety of library settings. This bibliography selects some useful material for guidance in developing or upgrading services to patrons with special needs. The bibliography is in alphabetical order by author, and has a subject index at the end.

BIBLIOGRAPHY

1. American Library Association. (1992). Resolution on poor people's services policy. In S. Berman and J. P. Danky (Eds.), *Alternative Library Literature 1990/1991* (pp. 110-111.) Jefferson, NC: McFarland & Co.

Rashelle S. Karp is Associate Professor, Department of Library Science, Clarion University of Pennsylvania, Clarion, PA 16214-1232. Email KARP@VAXA. Clarion.Edu. Patricia L. Horne is an MSLS candidate at Clarion University of Pennsylvania. She plans to seek employment in an academic or research library.

Dr. Rashelle S. Karp teaches in the areas of collection development, special libraries, and library services for disabled patrons.

[Haworth co-indexing entry note]: "Library Services to Traditionally Underserved Groups: An Annotated Bibliography." Karp, Rashelle S. and Patricia L. Horne. Co-published simultaneously in *The Reference Librarian* (The Haworth Press, Inc.) No. 53, 1996, pp. 63-96; and: *Reference Services for the Unserved* (ed: Fay Zipkowitz) The Haworth Press, Inc., 1996, pp. 63-96. Single or multiple copies of this article are available from The Haworth Document Delivery Service: [1-800-342-9678, 9:00 a.m. - 5:00 p.m. (EST)].

Reprinted from *Empowerment*, 2(1), Summer 1990, the policy is modeled on the ALA "Minority Concerns Policy" and promotes 15 activities to remove barriers to traditional library services for poor people. These activities include removal of fees and overdue charges, dissemination of appropriate information about and for low-income patrons, funding for legislative programs in support of low-income services, training for librarians on generating public funding to improve services to poor people, incorporation of low-income services into regular library budgets, increased public awareness of the importance of library services for poor people, community needs assessment, direct representation of poor people on library boards, training to sensitize library staff to issues affecting poor people, cooperation among librarians, and other proactive strategies.

2. Ayras, A. (1992). Library service for the Sámi population. *Scandinavian Public Library Quarterly, 25*(3), 17-21.

The oldest known population group in northern Scandinavia are the Sámi, who have their own language and dialects in which the emphasis is on speech, rather than writing. Research regarding library services to the Sámi reveals that although approximately 250 Sámi-language books were published between 1973 and 1989, librarians have found it difficult to acquire Sámi-language books because publishing is widely dispersed and poorly publicized. Language barriers also create problems in serving Sámi clientele in libraries. It is suggested that since inhabitants of the Sámi area use libraries as frequently as inhabitants of other areas in Scandinavia, librarians should take action to promote Sámi-language media (especially recordings and film) in order to facilitate the survival of the Sámi culture.

3. Barford, J. (1993). The key to empowerment: Inform 92. *Audiovisual Librarian, 19* (February), 45-50.

A conference (in Birmingham, England) focused on disseminating information to disabled individuals in Europe. Themes included the need for active involvement of disabled persons in the dissemination of information to other disabled persons, the empowering effect of information, the need for civil rights legislation in some

European countries, and the need for access to technology and current information.

4. Berman, S. and J. P. Danky (Eds.). (1992). *Alternative library literature, 1990/1991: A biennial anthology.* Jefferson, NC: McFarland & Co.

Begun in 1982/1983, the biennial anthology presents "a collection of rage, hope, insight, and inspiration" (p. xi) related to libraries and reprinted from various publications. Many articles deal with issues of library services to the underserved. In the 1990/1991 anthology, for example, the ALA "Poor People's Services Policy Resolution" and the Minnesota "Multicultural Resolution" are reprinted, as is an article dealing with the homeless and public libraries (these articles are indexed separately in this bibliography).

5. Broderick, D. M. (1992). Race. *Voice of Youth Advocates, 15*(August), 154,160.

Suggestions for encouraging greater involvement in libraries by black youth include fostering good library experiences for young children, arranging a graduation party for those leaving the children's room to introduce them to the young adult and adult sections, aggressively recruiting black youth to serve on library Youth Advisory Boards, and controlling one's own prejudicial or fearful reactions toward black youth in the library.

6. Bowie, M. M. (1992). Understanding and appreciating the unique needs of African Americans. In K. H. Latrobe and M. K. Laughlin (Eds.), *Multicultural aspects of library media programs* (pp. 26-44). Englewood, CO: Libraries Unlimited.

The author's perception of what it is to be African American is explored, the history of African Americans in the United States is summarized, persistent myths and misconceptions about African Americans are described, themes in African American literature and folklore are identified, and the library media specialist's role in helping African American students succeed in school is discussed. Suggestions for library media specialists include eliminating the designation of African American appreciation to a particular week or month, removing materials which endorse stereotypes from the collection, exploring different cultures' versions of folk tales, and providing materials and activities which promote positive self-concepts of African American students.

7. *Building effective program linkages: To establish a coordinated system of lifelong learning for adults with disabilities.* (1991). Washington, DC: Offices of Vocational and Adult Education and Special Education and Rehabilitative Services (ERIC Document Reproduction Service No. ED 337 618).

Proceedings of a joint conference of the Office of Special Education and Rehabilitative Services (OSERS) and the Office of Vocational and Adult Education (OVAE) held in Washington, D.C. (March 11-12, 1991) emphasized keeping disabled young people in school and preparing them for adulthood. The conference recommendations centered around five main themes: (1) improved interagency linkages at the Federal level; (2) dissemination of information about best practices and exemplary programs; (3) reduction of duplication by closer coordination of resources; (4) establishment of ongoing interagency cooperation; and (5) follow-up conferences to monitor progress and refine recommendations.

8. Caywood, C. (1993). Reaching out to gay teens. *School Library Journal, 39*(April), 50.

Librarians need to provide a variety of materials dealing with issues related to homosexuality, despite personal beliefs or community antagonisms against homosexuality. Gay teens, particularly, need such materials to validate their self-esteem and to reduce the potential for self-destructive behavior.

9. Cohen, F. (1992). Alternative library service serving special needs of patrons/homeborrower's program. *New Jersey Libraries, 25*(Summer), 16.

The Ocean County branch library provides a service for elderly and permanently or temporarily disabled patrons in which trained volunteers perform library "legwork" for homebound patrons.

10. Coombs, N. (1992). Electronic access to library systems for users with physical disabilities. In *The Public-access computer systems review, v1, 1990* (pp. 35-38). Chicago: Library & Information Technology Assn.

Electronic access for disabled library users involves provision of (1) adaptive hardware and appropriate software for use in the library; (2) remote electronic access to the library's collections; and (3) consultant services regarding electronic equipment.

11. Crosby, B. S. (1992). Multisensory programming: Fun and challenging. *Texas Libraries, 53*(Spring), 20-23.

Multisensory programs include slides, music, poetry, realia, and other opportunities for creative expression on a particular theme or era of recent history. They are designed not only to inform, but also to provide opportunities to reminisce, strengthen interpersonal bonds, and bridge generational gaps. Prepared program kits may be circulated by libraries. The programs are recommended for all people, but especially for older adults and children.

12. Dalton, P. I. (1992). ADA resources. *Library Personnel News, 6*(November/December), 6.

Described here are three resources emphasized at the 1992 President's Committee on Employment of People with Disabilities conference: "Willing to Act" (National Organization on Disability); *Job Accommodation Network Evaluation Report Executive Summary* (President's Committee on Employment of People with Disabilities); and *Implementing the Employer Provisions of the ADA* (President's Committee on Employment of People with Disabilities).

13. Davis, H. O. (1992). Map librarians, the international student, and ESL: Opportunity and challenge. *Bulletin (Special Libraries Association Geography and Map Division), 169*(September), 17-28.

The author discusses the use of maps in English as a Second Language (ESL) programs and the services that map librarians can provide for international students. Local maps, country and world maps, and maps of a student's native land may be incorporated into ESL programs to promote local orientation to the city and region, interest in English language resources, and confluent retention (improved learning through the presentation of concepts in multiple formats). Maps used in ESL programs should be simple and uncluttered, with a good legend and index. Map librarians can assist ESL instructors in choosing and understanding appropriate maps and can provide bibliographic instruction to international students in the library.

14. Davis, M. B. (1992). Developing a Native American Collection. *Wilson Library Bulletin*, 67(December), 33-37.

This guide to Native American literature provides information about titles and publishers in the areas of juvenile materials; encyclopedias; bibliographies and indexes; biographies; religion, mythology, and folklore; music and dance; literature; and federal Indian policy. A Native American collection should reflect the diversity of Native American groups, contain materials on all aspects of Native American life, emphasize contributions made by Native Americans to national and world communities, and portray Native Americans in the 20th century.

15. Davis, N. H. and Fitzgerald, P. (1993). Libraries and the homeless. *Library Journal*, 118(March 1), 27.

Suggestions for services to the expanding homeless population include providing social service referral information, job search and career guidance, educational/vocational course information, job applications, tax forms, driver's license applications, healthcare information, and current classified and help wanted sections. "Crisis literacy" programs and library-based tutoring services are also suggested.

16. Evans, G. E. (1992). Needs analysis and collection development policies for culturally diverse populations. *Collection Building*, 11(4), 16-27.

Sources of information about culturally diverse communities include U.S. census tapes, the National Opinion Research Center of

Chicago, the Ethnic Materials Information Exchange (EMIE), local school district central offices, local Chambers of Commerce, and city planning offices. Sources which provide information beyond statistics include ethnic community events, religious organizations, social service organizations, local merchants, and formal and informal community leaders.

17. Farmer, L. S. J. (1992). Understanding and appreciating the unique needs of Asian-Pacific Americans. In K. H. Latrobe and M. K. Laughlin (Eds.), *Multicultural aspects of library media programs* (pp. 7-25). Englewood, CO: Libraries Unlimited.

Asian-Pacific immigrants to the United States face cultural and value conflicts with dominant American cultures, but the common perception of Asian-Pacific Americans as model immigrants may mask their needs for help in adapting. The immigration history and educational issues relating to these groups are discussed. Suggestions for helping Asian-Pacific students in the school library include providing library orientation in the student's original language, providing additional instruction in the use and structure of the card catalog and other reference tools, and incorporating multisensory materials whenever possible.

18. Fersh, D. and Thomas, P. W. (1993). *Complying with the American with Disabilities Act: A guidebook for management and people with disabilities.* Westport, CT: Quorum.

Written in non-legal language, this answers the questions of business people, people with disabilities, and the general public regarding the ADA. It outlines the purpose and provisions of the ADA and thoroughly explores the implications of the Act for businesses and places of public accommodation. Issues of awareness and enforcement are also discussed. A directory of Federal and National Association resources is included.

19. Foos, D. D. and Pack, N. C. (1992). ADA case studies and exercises. In D. D. Foos and N. C. Pack (Eds.), *How libraries must comply with the Americans with Disabilities Act (ADA)* (pp. 112-132). Phoenix, AZ: Oryx.

Hypothetical cases posed and discussed include a new deputy director trying to stimulate ADA awareness under a director nearing retirement, a researcher placed on long term disability leave who requires special services from his company's special library in order to receive current information in his field, a transsexual library employee requesting use of the female restroom facilities, a Library maintenance worker who develops a severe health problem, and the retention of a food-handler in a city library's cafeteria who has tested HIV-positive.

20. Frederiksen, L. (1992). Health and culture: An interdisciplinary project. *Scandinavian Public Library Ouarterly, 25*(3), 8-9.

In an experimental project in the municipality of Ringsed, Denmark, a consultant for the elderly and a part-time librarian were hired to organize community activities to meet the social and informational needs of the elderly. The librarian's tasks included offering background material for workshops and organizing cultural activities such as the showing of films, visits to museums and libraries, ballad singing, and lectures. Use of the library by elderly borrowers has continued long past the duration of the project.

21. Full and equal access: Americans with Disabilities Act. (1992). *Unabashed Librarian, 82*, 25-31.

This reprint of an article from *Illinois Libraries*, October 1991, summarizes Titles II (public entities) and III (public accommodations) of the ADA and their implications for libraries. Defined are "individual with a disability," "accessibility," and "alteration." Also included are a set of ADA questions and answers and a list of sources for more information about the ADA.

22. Ganfield, D. (1992). Books by mail at the Ocean County Library. *New Jersey Libraries*, (Summer), 15.

In its books by mail service to the homebound, the library began paying postage both ways in 1991. Popularity of this service has since increased. Patrons have access to the entire collection.

23. Gregg, A. (1992). On her blindness: Reflections on the use of spoken word cassettes from the public library. *Australian Library Journal, 41*(May), 129-132.

The author relates her reliance on and the pleasures derived from spoken word cassettes during her recovery from cataract surgery. Also discussed are the frustrations she experienced because of inadequate labeling for the sight impaired. Often, bibliographical information was available only in small print on the cassette case, and titles of poems and other short works were not announced prior to their reading.

24. Gunde, M. G. (1991/1992). Working with the Americans with Disabilities Act. *Library Journal, 116*(December), 99-100; 117 (May 1), 41-42; 117(December), 90-91.

Frequently asked questions about making libraries comply with the ADA are discussed in this three part question and answer series.

25. Hall, C. B. (1992). Books or walls of brick: Literacy in Alaskan libraries. *Sourdough, 29*(Fall), 9-10.

Fairbanks North Star Borough Library Literacy Project provides services for adults studying basic skills or English as a Second Language (ESL). A coordinator recruits and trains tutors, obtains special materials, and conducts tours and workshops. Projects have included creating information packets for adult students and tutors, distributing a listing of local Adult Basic Education and ESL agencies, and establishing eleven literacy libraries throughout the borough.

26. Hall, P. A. (1992). Peanuts: A note on intercultural communication. *Journal of Academic Librarianship, 18*(September), 211-213.

Librarians must guard against cultural bias by becoming aware of cultural differences in communication patterns. These differences, which may be much more subtle than language barriers, pose serious obstructions to effective communication with patrons of different cultures.

27. Harrington, J. N. (1993). The need for cultural diversity in preschool services. *Journal of Youth Services in Libraries, 6*(Winter), 175-179.

Suggestions for incorporating positive multicultural images and experiences into library services for preschoolers include making programs, services, staffs, and collections reflect the diversity in the community and offering workshops and information services to early childhood professionals serving minority children.

28. Hernández-Delgado, J. L. (1992). Pura Tersa Belpré, storyteller and pioneer Puerto Rican librarian. *Library Quarterly, 62*(October), 425-440.

Belpré was the first Puerto Rican librarian hired by the New York Public Library. Her work as a children's librarian, author, and teller of stories and Puerto Rican folk tales is described.

29. *How libraries must comply with the Americans with Disabilities Act (ADA).* (1992). D. D. Foos and N. C. Pack (Eds.). Phoenix, AZ: Oryx.

Topics covered include a summary of the ADA and its general implications for libraries, steps in planning the implementation of the ADA in the library, the ADA's impact upon school library media centers, legal implications of the ADA, hypothetical case studies, and a quick guide to the ADA.

30. Humes, B. A. and Lyons, C. A. (1992). *Library literacy program: Description of funded projects 1990: Title VI, Library Services and Construction Act.* Washington, DC: Office of Educational Research and Improvement, U.S. Dept. of Education (ERIC Document Reproduction Service No. ED 344 614).

This booklet provides a description of adult literacy programs in public libraries funded by grants made available through Title VI of the Library Services and Construction Act (LSCA) in fiscal year 1990. Part I provides a general list of activities incorporated into literacy programs and assigns a code to each of these activities. Part II lists each library which received funds through LSCA Title VI in 1990 along with the amount received (up to $25,000) and the activity codes from Part I which describe the program. Part III gives statistical information about LSCA Title VI funding in 1990. The list is useful for identifying library literacy programs providing specific services and for generating ideas for starting or expanding a literacy program.

31. Ip, L.-N. L. (1992). Public library services to older Pennsylvanians: A decade review. *Public Library Quarterly, 12(1),* 41-61.

Results of the 1989 survey of public libraries in Pennsylvania support several positive conclusions: (1) public libraries provide services for older people although most do not have written policy statements for such services; (2) leadership in this area is provided by District Library Centers and Headquarters of the state library system; (3) public libraries identify older people who may have special needs and provide special services to meet these needs; and (4) public libraries employ older volunteer workers. Negative conclusions supported by the survey included data revealing that public libraries (1) do not have enough librarians trained to provide services to older people; (2) provide few projects and programs for the elderly; (3) put less effort into recruitment of older users; and (4) are less likely to cosponsor services with community agencies for older people. Recommendations for improving services include requesting additional funds from parent institutions, providing more training workshops for librarians who serve older populations, cosponsoring more services for older people with community agencies, providing more outreach services to older people in remote areas, making use of local media and social agencies to publicize library programs, and continuing to recruit librarians committed to serving older populations.

32. Jackson, S. (1992). A puff of breath, a tilt of the head and presto! . . . it's a toy library for children with disabilities. *Mississippi Libraries, 56*(Fall), 76-78.

The Toy Library-Coast serves patrons in three Mississippi counties by lending toys which are specially designed for children with disabilities and by instructing children and their families on the use of these toys.

33. Karrenbrock, M. H. (1992). The impact of the ADA upon school library media centers. In D. D. Foos and N. C. Pack (Eds.), *How libraries must comply with the Americans with Disabilities Act (ADA)* (pp. 70-88). Phoenix, AZ: Oryx.

Following a summary of the legislative history regarding persons with disabilities prior to the ADA, the author suggests that in light of legislation already in place, the ADA will have little direct impact upon school library media centers. Indirect effects of the ADA, however, will include an increased public awareness of the rights of disabled individuals, increased employment of persons with disabilities in school library media centers, and an increased number of program self-evaluations. Opportunities presented by the ADA include increased demands on school library media specialists to (1) disseminate information about people with disabilities; (2) develop flexible policies to meet the needs of people with disabilities; (3) foster the development of positive attitudes toward people with disabilities through education; and (4) form partnerships among educators, students, and parents.

34. Koppa, A. (1992). Library service for the elderly: Experiences and plans in Tampere. *Scandinavian Public Library Quarterly, 25*(3), 4-7.

A librarian in Tampere, Finland, shares her vision of library services to the elderly in a time of economic recession and budget crunch. Suggestions include keeping small familiar branch libraries and bookmobiles running, maintaining large print and talking book collections, and developing delivery services for homebound patrons.

35. Library of Congress. National Library Service for the Blind and Physically Handicapped. (19–). *Library resources for the blind and physically handicapped; a directory with FY 1990 statistics on readership, circulation, budget, staff, and collections.* Washington, DC: Library of Congress.

This annual directory of regional and subregional libraries for the blind and physically handicapped in the United States, Puerto Rico, the Virgin Islands, and Guam provides information about each library's budget, staff, collections, readership, and circulation of recorded disc, braille, and recorded cassette materials.

36. Liu, Z. (1993). Difficulties and characteristics of students from developing countries in using American libraries. *College & Research Libraries, 54*(January), 25-31.

A survey of 54 international graduate and undergraduate students (predominantly Asian) at the University of California, Berkeley, indicates that these students experience problems due to their lack of English proficiency, poor understanding of American library organization and procedures, unfamiliarity with copyright laws, and inexperience with large online databases. Students studying natural sciences had fewer problems than those studying the humanities, and students who were more proficient in English or whose home countries were strongly influenced by American culture had fewer problems than other international students.

37. Massis, B. (1993). Libraries for the Blind pre-conference seminar on the furtherance of literacy for the visually handicapped in developing countries, 24-28 August 1992. *IFLA Journal, 19*(1), 107-108.

Conferees at the 1992 IFLA Conference concluded that access to alternative formats could be improved through more effective use of local organizations, development of a directory of Asian language materials in alternative formats, inclusion of alternative formats in bibliographies of Asian national libraries, and elimination of postal/customs restrictions on the delivery of materials in alternative formats. It was also suggested that there be an All-Indian conference to promote cooperation between organizations serving the visually handicapped, and that more training for librarians serving the visually impaired be provided through programs and sub-regional seminars.

38. Mates, B. T. (1992). Adaptive technology makes libraries "people friendly." *Computers in Libraries, 12*(November), 20-25.

Suggestions for adapting library services for people with disabilities include implementing staff sensitivity training, providing good lighting, and purchasing low-tech devices before purchasing high-tech devices. For those libraries that have the resources to purchase high-tech adaptive technology, the following suggestions are given: do it all at one time; develop a written policy manual; purchase items which serve the most users for the least amount of money; comparison shop; be sure instructions for the use of devices are available in braille, large print, or recorded format; advertise the devices' accessibility; and constantly reevaluate services. CD-ROMs with alternative output and reading machines are also discussed.

39. _____. (1991). *Library technology for visually and physically impaired patrons*. Westport, CT: Heckler.

Access to library materials can be improved through the use of large-print, braille, audio output, optical character recognition (OCR) systems, keyboards, processing information without a keyboard, and technology for the deaf and hearing impaired. The author provides information about specific products and their prices. Approaches to implementing adaptive technology in the library and the probable future growth of adaptive technology are also discussed. Appendices include a directory of vendors and distributors of technological devices for the blind and physically handicapped, a listing of CD-ROM titles that translate into special format, a directory of bulletin boards addressing the needs of disabled persons, and a discussion of funding sources for adaptive equipment.

40. McDaniel, J. A. (1992). They can't hear us does not mean we can't serve them. *Journal of Library Administration, 16*(4), 131-141.

Equipment to facilitate use of the library by hearing impaired patrons includes telecommunication devices for the deaf (TDDs), caption decoders for closed caption television programs, induction loop systems or FM systems, and alarm systems which include flashing lights and sound cues. Helpful materials include reference materials that specifically address the needs of hearing impaired patrons, reading materials commensurate with reading levels of hearing impaired patrons, and captioned films and videos. Activities that facilitate use of the library include reduction of background noise, provision of interpreters at programs, and inclusion of members of the deaf community in community assessment.

41. McNulty, T. (1993). Reference service for students with disabilities: Desktop braille publishing in the academic library. *Reference Services Review, 21*(1), 37-43.

Processes and equipment needed to produce all essential information in braille for New York University's first deaf/blind student included obtaining materials from sources such as the American Printing House of the Blind (APH), use of the Kurzweil Personal Reader to scan printed material and write it to an ASCII file, use of the Duxbury Braille Translater to translate the ASCII file into braille, and use of the VersaPoint Braille Embosser to print braille copy. The article concludes with information on obtaining the products discussed and a brief directory of national organizations which provide information on braille and adaptive technology.

42. Metoyer-Duran, C. (1993). Cross-cultural research in ethnolinguistic communities: Methodological-considerations. *Public Libraries, 32*(January/February), 18-25.

Sampling issues in conducting research in culturally diverse communities include difficulties obtaining a representative sample and difficulties defining culturally diverse communities. Public librarians seeking to conduct research should concentrate only on the variable(s) of greatest importance to them. In order to maximize participation in the study, librarians should (1) cooperate with ethnic community organizations to promote the study; (2) employ culturally diverse members of the community to contact potential participants; (3) offer compensation to participants; and (4) provide a summary of findings to participants in their preferred language. Other recommended strategies: using experienced researchers to conduct the study; emphasizing the importance of culturally diverse communities by promoting their participation and by using bilingual researchers and instruments; developing a good sampling strategy; conducting pretests; considering the convenience of the participants; and disseminating findings widely throughout the community.

43. _____ . (1993). The information and referral process in culturally diverse communities. *RQ*, *32*(Spring), 359-371.

A 1990 California State Library study of the information seeking behavior of 129 ethnolinguistic information providers in California found that, while these American Indian, Chinese, Japanese, Korean, and Latino gatekeepers have a positive view of the public library, they do not see the library as an information and referral center. Strengthening the link between these community gatekeepers and the public library could promote an influential advocacy on behalf of the library. Suggestions to strengthen this link include developing selective dissemination of information (SDI) services to meet the needs of the gatekeepers, becoming familiar with other institutional sources used by gatekeepers, and providing services in languages appropriate to culturally diverse community groups.

44. Morris-Guerin, G. (1992). Innovative approaches at Hasting District Libraries. *New Zealand Libraries*, *47* (December), 70-71.

The library's recent efforts to meet the demands of biculturalism and to update services to teenagers include creating separate sections for teenagers and for Maori populations. In addition, items in the Maori section have special labels, and signage is bilingual. The library has since witnessed an increase in use of the library by Maori people.

45. _____ . (1992). Native American library and information services. *Government Information Quarterly, 9*(3), 359-362.

National priorities for improving library and information services for Native Americans, as expressed at the 1991 White House Conference on Library and Information Services, include the collection of data relating to tribal library and information services, the establishment of Federal depositories at reservation libraries, and the inclusion of tribal libraries in electronic networks.

46. Minnesota multicultural resolution. (1992). In S. Berman and J. P. Danky (Eds.), *Alternative library literature. 1990/1991* (p. 131). Jefferson, NC: McFarland & Co.

The resolution includes plans to establish a multicultural resource network for accessing and delivering resources and programs that are multicultural, gender-fair, and disability-inclusive; encouragements to Minnesota librarians to insure that the materials they collect reflect the state's cultural diversity; recognition that adequate federal and state funds must be allocated to support these services; and the recommendation that opportunities and financial assistance be made available to encourage potential authors and artists from Minnesota minority cultures.

47. *Multicultural aspects of library media programs.* (1992). K. H. Latrobe and M. K. Laughlin (Eds.). Englewood, CO: Libraries Unlimited.

Designed as a reference tool for school library media specialists concerned with multicultural issues, the work is a collection of both theoretical and practical readings on the topic. Main sections include unique perspectives on the needs of particular groups, discussions of multicultural curricula in relation to school library media programs, and multicultural collection development issues. Authors were chosen on the basis of their experience or expertise with the topic, and each article includes a reference list and/or bibliography. A comprehensive glossary and index are also included.

48. New York Library Association. (1992). Guidelines for libraries serving patrons with a hearing impairment: Prepared by the Roundtable for Libraries Serving Special Populations. *Library Trends, 41*(Summer), 164-172.

These official guidelines, excerpted from NYLA's 1987 *Guidelines for Libraries Serving Persons with a Hearing Impairment or a Visual Impairment*, include a self assessment instrument for libraries serving persons with hearing impairments.

49. Nierman, J. (1992). Copyright law affects service for blind and physically handicapped. *Library of Congress Information Bulletin, 51*(November 16), 493.

The efforts of the National Library Service for the Blind and Physically Handicapped (NLS) to make materials available to blind and physically handicapped persons are affected by U.S. copyright law since approval must be obtained from each book's copyright holder before it may be produced in a special format. NLS adds about 2,000 books a year to its special format collection and in reproducing these works, the NLS must protect copyright holders from piracy.

50. Norton, M. J. (1992). Effective bibliographic instruction for deaf and hearing-impaired college students. *Library Trends, 41* (Summer), 118-150.

Suggestions are made concerning the use of visual and hands-on instruction, written library instruction materials, and special equipment and technology to facilitate communication. An appendix includes the "National Institute for the Deaf (NTID) Guide to Wallace Library" as a model for printed instructional material.

51. Norton, M. J. and Kovalik, G. L. (1992). Libraries serving an underserved population: Deaf and hearing-impaired patrons. *Library Trends, 41*(Summer), 1-176.

This is a special issue devoted to library services to deaf and hearing-impaired persons. Topics include past and present library services, overcoming communication barriers, collection development, information retrieval, deaf characters in fiction, sharing literature with deaf children, standards for library media centers in schools for the deaf, captioned films, bibliographic instruction for deaf and hearing-impaired college students, and New York state guidelines for libraries serving persons with a hearing impairment.

52. Odien, J. M. (1992). Standards for library media centers in schools for the deaf: An updated perspective. *Library Trends*, *41* (Summer), 85-99.

The author provides a historical overview of the development of national standards for library media centers in schools for the deaf, reports on the influence of standards on the profession, and calls for a reevaluation of the standards which would consider the whole range of hearing-impaired learners and their educational needs within a greater variety of placement options.

53. O'Donnell, R. E. (1992). Planning to implement the ADA in the library. In D. D. Foos and N. C. Pack (Eds.), *How libraries must comply with the Americans with Disabilities Act (ADA)*, (pp. 32-69). Phoenix, AZ: Oryx.

This six step implementation model involves gathering information, appointing a coordinator, conducting self-evaluation, formulating plans, implementing plans, and maintaining services. Emphasis is on listening to library patrons with disabilities.

54. Pack, N. C. and Foos, D. D. (1992). Library compliance with the Americans with Disabilities Act. *RQ*, *32*(Winter), 255-267.

The authors summarize (1) Title I (Employment), Title II (Public Services), Title III (Public Accommodations), and Title IV (Telecommunications) of the ADA as they apply to libraries; (2) documented library efforts to comply with the ADA; and (3) legal caselaw related to the ADA. Suggestions for library compliance with the ADA include gathering information about the ADA; designating an ADA coordinator; evaluating current library policies, programs, services, and facilities in terms of the ADA; implementing necessary changes; training all library staff in ADA compliance; and obtaining feedback from library users with disabilities.

55. Page, C. (1992). 'I can read but I can't turn the pages.' *Electronic Library, 10*(December), 333-337.

The Nuffield Interactive Book System (NIBS) is an interactive text delivery system implemented in 1990 at Hereward College (UK) for students with physical and sensory disabilities. The system is designed to facilitate reading for students with motor disabilities, loss of limb control, or loss of limbs. The NIBS allows browsing of textual material and viewing of the structural map of material. Its capabilities include hypertext facilities, key word/phrase searching, viewing and enlarging, highlighting, restructuring of highlighted material, and annotating. Users have reacted positively to NIBS, and it is becoming available to other colleges in the UK and Europe and to able bodied students.

56. Patterson, L. (1992). Native American library services: Reclaiming the past, designing the future. *Wilson Library Bulletin, 67*(December), 28;119.

This summary of the evolution of native American libraries since the 1970s describes the impact of legislation such as the Indian Self-Determination and Education Assistance Act (1975), the Higher Education Act Title II-B, LSCA Title IV, and the National Indian Omnibus Library Bill. Goals for the future include amending LSCA Title IV and passing legislation to provide continuing education and training for Native American library professionals and paraprofessionals.

57. _____ . (1992). Understanding and appreciating the unique needs of Native Americans. In K. H. Latrobe and M. K. Laughlin (Eds.), *Multicultural aspects of library media programs* (pp. 54-60). Englewood, CO: Libraries Unlimited.

Many common cultural values of Native Americans and the ways in which they may conflict with dominant values are described (e.g., cooperation, modesty, placidity, generosity, and avoidance of eye contact). Suggestions for educational systems and library media programs include identifying and eliminating stereotypes, appreciating cultural differences in values, and providing multicultural education. Three multicultural activities for the library media program involving the generalization, analysis, and evaluation of information are recommended.

58. Pelzman, F. National support for Native American libraries: The NCLIS commitment. *Wilson Library Bulletin, 67*(December), 29-32.

Field hearings conducted by the National Commission on Libraries and Information Science (NCLIS) have found that Native Americans are underserved with regard to libraries partly because some communities lack funds even for bookmobile services, and many tribal leaders do not place a priority on library services. Rampant illiteracy and the preservation of tribal archives are key issues.

59. Peterson, J. (1992). Nordic cooperation on video for deaf people. *Scandinavian Public Library Quarterly, 25*(3), 13-14.

From 1986 to 1988, the Nordic countries instituted a program in which videos for the deaf produced in each country were made available to deaf viewers in the other Nordic countries by distributing copies of the videos to Nordic video institutions. This program was not sufficiently successful, and a new program was proposed which was similar to the interlibrary loan programs which facilitate distribution of talking books for the blind. It was proposed that the Swedish Library of Talking Books and Braille (TPB) become the central distributor of Swedish videos for the deaf in the Nordic countries.

60. Pilger, M. A. (1992). *Multicultural projects index: Things to make and do to celebrate festivals, cultures, and holidays around the world.* Englewood, CO: Libraries Unlimited.

This index provides references to books and parts of books which describe crafts, special days and festivals, recipes, games, and historical projects. Most items are indexed under their own names and under the country or culture of origin. Each reference includes the subject, a brief description, a book number from the bibliography, and page numbers.

61. Reed, S. G. (1992). Breaking through: Effective reference mediation for nontraditional public library users. *The Reference Librarian, 37*, 109-119.

Suggestions for providing fair reference service to mentally impaired patrons include keeping a positive attitude toward patrons and their requests, assessing a patron's comprehension and ability levels, spending enough time to deliver adequate service, finding developmentally appropriate material, and helping a patron interpret information. Suggestions for providing fair reference service to illiterate and newly literate adults include establishing a feeling of comfort and trust; being attentive to clues of illiteracy and handling these tactfully; spending enough time to ensure that a patron's need has been met; and providing alternative formats such as audio, video, and children's works. It is further suggested that libraries and other community agencies take aggressive action to assess and mediate potential patrons' problems in a broader way, rather than just on a one-to-one basis.

62. Sarkodie-Mensah, K. (1992). Dealing with international students in a multicultural era. *Journal of Academic Librarianship, 18*(September), 214-216.

In order to improve communication with international students, librarians must develop an awareness of the speech patterns of different cultures, listen to the words students say rather than their intonation, use tact at all times, develop foreign language skills, and learn about different cultures.

63. Sarokin, H. L. (1992). ALA conference: Judge Sarokin speaks. *Newsletter on Intellectual Freedom, 41*(September), 134-135.

Judge Sarokin speaks on issues related to the controversial Kreimer v. Morristown case involving a homeless man and his ouster from a New Jersey public library for disruptive behavior.

Sarokin defends his position that public library policies which allow a librarian to ask someone to leave the library must be made more precise.

64. Schuler, C. and Meck, S. (1992). Sharing traditional and contemporary literature with deaf children. *Library Trends, 41* (Summer), 61-84.

Considerations in choosing and sharing traditional and contemporary fictional literature with a deaf child are discussed: (1) a story without too much complexity should be selected, and emphasis during presentation should be given to illustrations and visual comfort; (2) the teller should use the story to enrich the emotional life of the child; (3) the teller must set the scene so the child understands the context of the story; (4) the child must be emotionally and intellectually prepared for the content of the story; (5) the teller should relate the story to the real world so the child has better access to it; (6) an edition with quality text and illustrations should be chosen, and the illustrations should not be merely ornamental but should reinforce the text; (7) American Sign Language (ASL) should be used rather than Signed English; and (8) the story may be used to teach valuable moral lessons, but the teller should guard against communicating stereotypes. Suggestions for collection development and physical considerations for a deaf audience are also given. Includes a bibliography of suggested books as well as other bibliographical references.

65. Scott, B. A. (1993). Literacy activities in Florida's public libraries. *Florida Librarian, 36* (January), 8-9.

This selective directory lists Florida libraries which (1) provide literacy instructional programs; (2) participate in local literacy coalitions by providing meeting and office space, materials, referral services, publicity, recruitment, and/or planning services; or (3) provide individualized computer-assisted literacy programs. The nature of a literacy program in a library is briefly discussed, and contact information for becoming involved in the literacy efforts in Florida is given.

66. Seeking a balance: Patrons and policies. (1992). *New Jersey Libraries*, 25(Fall)', 2-24.

This special issue discusses aspects of the Kreimer v. Morristown case (a homeless man was ousted from a New Jersey public library for disruptive behavior) and its implications for public libraries. Article topics include an analysis of the New Jersey Library Association's response to the case, the outcomes of the case as viewed by one of Kreimer's court-appointed attorneys, and a description of the case and its background as viewed by the director of the Joint Free Public Library of Morristown and Morris Township. Additional articles discuss the legal, social, and library service issues involved in establishing codes of conduct for library patrons and propose ALA guidelines for the development of such codes.

67. Shipp, C. J. (1993). Adventures in Kwangu. *School Library Journal*, 39(January), 39.

A gameboard based on African folklore stimulated a children's reading program for African-American History Month at a Chicago branch library. For each book read, children earned a turn at the gameboard and five wooden beads to string into a necklace. Children also performed renditions of traditional African and African-American folktales to complement the highly successful program.

68. Smale, R. (1992). Australian university library services for visually impaired students: Results of a survey. *Australian Library Journal*, 41(August), 199-212.

Smale found that there are still many barriers to information retrieval and learning in higher education for visually impaired students. Common problems include inadequate staffing devoted to the visually impaired; insufficient availability of catalog, reference, and other materials in alternative formats; lack of availability of reading aids; and problems with building design. Another significant finding was that many library staff members and visually impaired patrons are not aware of the services that libraries do offer for visually impaired patrons.

69. Stilwell, C. (1992). The resource centre forums: Democratic and alternative information networks for South Africa. *International Information and Library Review, 24*(September), 213-220.

In the 1980s and 90s, many resource centers have been formed in South Africa to meet the resource and information needs of underserved non-white populations. The Transkei Fieldworkers' Network Resource Centre, set up in May 1990, serves the member organization of the Transkei Fieldworkers' Network. The Natal Resource Centre Forum was formed in 1988 to collect and distribute accurate historical and political information. The short-lived Community Resource Centre Training Project (CRCTP) was instituted to train information workers. The Transvaal Resource Centre Network began in 1989, and the Sekhukhuneland Educational Projects Forum was formed in 1991 to link different projects in the area. Despite the many difficulties these organizations have had, the Resource Centre Forums are represented on the National Education Policy Investigation.

70. Story, R. M. F. (1992). Understanding and appreciating the unique needs of Mexican Americans. In K. H. Latrobe and M. K. Laughlin (Eds.), *Multicultural aspects of library media programs* (pp. 45-53). Englewood, CO: Libraries Unlimited.

After summarizing the history of Mexican Americans, the author outlines current demographics and discusses the role of school library media centers in helping Mexican Americans succeed in school. Suggestions include integrating Mexican-American culture into the whole curriculum, collecting many library materials in Spanish as well as English materials about Hispanic cultures, disseminating relevant information to teachers and administrators, and obtaining reviewing sources of Spanish-language books. Poetry and short stories are emphasized as being particularly appealing to Mexican-American children.

71. Stout, M. A. (1992). Library use of adaptive technology for the disabled. In W. Crawford (Ed.), *LITA yearbook 1992* (pp. 11-12). Chicago: Library & Information Technology Assn.

This report of the 1992 ALA Conference address of Dr. Alan Brightman (based on his book, *Independence Day: Designing Computer Solutions for Individuals with Disability*), discusses Brightman's analysis of Apple computer technology for use by disabled individuals, and his common sense, reality-based approaches.

72. Sumner, M. A. (1991). *Safari adventures: A bibliography for young readers, preschool through junior high.* Daytona Beach, FL: Bureau of Library Services for the Blind and Physically Handicapped (ERIC Document Reproduction Service No. ED 353 985).

Prepared in conjunction with the State Library of Florida's Summer Library Program for 1991, this bibliography provides citations to books in alternative formats that fit the safari theme of the program. The bibliography is divided into six safaris–African, jungle, animal, dinosaur, distant, and backyard. Citations to books related to the topic of each safari are then divided into braille, cassette, and recorded disc formats. Citations include a brief description of the book and recommended grade levels. The books listed were either produced in Florida or can be obtained from the National Library Service for the Blind and Physically Handicapped (NLS). Approximately 400 titles are listed.

73. Szekely, C. (1993). Library services for Maori people. *Wilson Library Bulletin, 67*(April), 46-48.

The Maori are New Zealand's largest cultural minority. Difficulties in providing Maori-language materials in libraries include a shortage of such materials, lack of reviews, and lack of promotion. Maori research needs include the need for materials to support genealogical research and the need for information relating to Waitangi Tribunal claims. Efforts to make libraries more welcoming to the Maori include the development of a Maori subject heading thesaurus by the National Library, microfiching important Maori historical records, the hiring of Maori to work in libraries (although this is sparse), encouragement of Maori to gain professional library qualifications through scholarships, and the commissioning by the New Zealand Library and Information Association of a researcher to gather information on Maori library usage. Despite these efforts, there is prevailing apathy within the library profession about services to the Maori.

74. Taylor, Rhonda. (1992). Profiles: Four Native American libraries. *Wilson Library Bulletin, 67*(December), 38-39.

Highlights of these four diverse libraries include preservation of tribal history and culture at the Colorado River Indian Tribes Public Library/Archives in La Paz county, Arizona; youth services at Fort Berthold Reservation Public Library in New Town, North Dakota; educational services at the Nisqually Tribal Library outside Olympia, Washington; and outreach services at The Navaho Nation Library System which serves residents of the Navaho Reservation in Utah, Arizona, and New Mexico.

75. Vendors and distributors of technological devices for the blind and physically handicapped. (1992). *Computers in Libraries, 12*(November), 31-34.

This alphabetical listing of vendors and distributors in the United States and Canada provides addresses and phone numbers, as well as a listing of sponsors of bulletin boards for disabled individuals.

76. Wood, N. (1992). The vision shared. *Audiovisual Librarian, 18*(August), 178-182.

Needs expressed by speakers at the visually impaired persons services seminar in York, England (May 1992) included needs for improved library staff training, provision of appropriate equipment, better legislation and government funding for the visually impaired, more publishing of large print books, more widespread use of recent technologies, inclusion of visually impaired persons in management services, and better assessment of community needs.

77. Yee, H.M. (1991). *Cross cultural studies for teacher-librarians: A project funded under the Multicultural and Cross-cultural Supplementation Program (MACSP): Final report: With the assistance of Len Cairns and Rhonda Renwick.* Churchill Vic., Australia: School of Education, Monash University College Gippsland (ERIC Document Reproduction Service No. ED 340 352).

This report (1) outlines the history of multiculturalism in Australia; (2) addresses the role of school libraries in a multicultural society; (3) presents the results of surveys conducted regarding relevant literature and tertiary institutions offering training courses for school librarians, state departments of education, school librarians, and students of school librarianship; (4) provides seven lesson modules for cross-cultural learning; and (5) proposes guidelines for developing cross-cultural collections.

78. Yuhasz, L. (1992). The Lighthouse at Community Medical Center aging resource center. *New Jersey Libraries*, *25*(Summer), 14-15.

The collections and services provided by this library are described. Resources include educational materials for older adults, caregivers and families, health professionals, gerontologists, and students. Materials have been compiled to help elderly populations meet the challenges of aging.

INDEX

(Numbers refer to entry numbers, not to pages)

Index

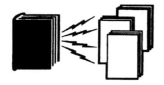

Haworth
DOCUMENT DELIVERY
SERVICE

This valuable service provides a single-article order form for any article from a Haworth journal.

- *Time Saving:* No running around from library to library to find a specific article.
- *Cost Effective:* All costs are kept down to a minimum.
- *Fast Delivery:* Choose from several options, including same-day FAX.
- *No Copyright Hassles:* You will be supplied by the original publisher.
- *Easy Payment:* Choose from several easy payment methods.

Open Accounts Welcome for . . .
- Library Interlibrary Loan Departments
- Library Network/Consortia Wishing to Provide Single-Article Services
- Indexing/Abstracting Services with Single Article Provision Services
- Document Provision Brokers and Freelance Information Service Providers

---

MAIL or *FAX* THIS ENTIRE ORDER FORM TO:

Haworth Document Delivery Service
The Haworth Press, Inc.
10 Alice Street
Binghamton, NY 13904-1580

or FAX: 1-800-895-0582
or CALL: 1-800-342-9678
9am-5pm EST

PLEASE SEND ME PHOTOCOPIES OF THE FOLLOWING SINGLE ARTICLES:

1) Journal Title: _____

  Vol/Issue/Year:_____ Starting & Ending Pages:_____

  Article Title:_____

  _____

2) Journal Title: _____

  Vol/Issue/Year:_____ Starting & Ending Pages:_____

  Article Title:_____

  _____

3) Journal Title: _____

  Vol/Issue/Year:_____ Starting & Ending Pages:_____

  Article Title:_____

  _____

4) Journal Title: _____

  Vol/Issue/Year:_____ Starting & Ending Pages:_____

  Article Title:_____

  _____

(See other side for Costs and Payment Information)

COSTS: Please figure your cost to order quality copies of an article.

1. Set-up charge per article: $8.00

    ($8.00 × number of separate articles) _____

2. Photocopying charge for each article:

    1-10 pages: $1.00 _____

    11-19 pages: $3.00 _____

    20-29 pages: $5.00 _____

    30+ pages: $2.00/10 pages _____

3. Flexicover (optional): $2.00/article _____

4. Postage & Handling: US: $1.00 for the first article/

    $.50 each additional article _____

    Federal Express: $25.00 _____

    Outside US: $2.00 for first article/

    $.50 each additional article _____

5. Same-day FAX service: $.35 per page _____

    GRAND TOTAL: _____

METHOD OF PAYMENT: (please check one)

❑ Check enclosed   ❑ Please ship and bill. PO # _____
    (sorry we can ship and bill to bookstores only! All others must pre-pay)

❑ Charge to my credit card: ❑ Visa; ❑ MasterCard; ❑ Discover;
    ❑ American Express;

Account Number:_____ Expiration date:_____

Signature: X_____

Name: _____ Institution: _____

Address: _____

_____

City: _____ State:_____ Zip:_____

Phone Number: _____ FAX Number: _____

MAIL or *FAX* THIS ENTIRE ORDER FORM TO:

Haworth Document Delivery Service	**or FAX:** 1-800-895-0582
The Haworth Press, Inc.	**or CALL:** 1-800-342-9678
10 Alice Street	9am-5pm EST)
Binghamton, NY 13904-1580	